# What People Are Saying About

## *The Mindful Medium*

Alison puts her experience as a teacher to good effect when it comes to explaining the principles and practice of relaxation techniques, guided meditation, and psychic awareness. Aware of the stumbling blocks in the path of the novice, Alison also skilfully steers the more advanced practitioners towards developing their own style. Always clear and always good humoured, the aspiring practitioner would be hard pushed to find a better guide to this often confusing area.

**Dr Ian Rubenstein**, GP and author of *Consulting Spirit: A Doctor's Experience with Practical Mediumship*

*The Mindful Medium* is an essential tool for all budding mediums on the next stages of their spiritual path. I found Alison's help invaluable and her writing inspiring, helping me to move deeper into spiritualism and connect with my true essence. I can't recommend Alison and her words enough.

**Halina Watts**, freelance showbiz editor

# The Mindful Medium

## A Practical Guide to Spirituality

# The Mindful Medium

## A Practical Guide to Spirituality

Alison Grey

**6TH
BOOKS**

Winchester, UK
Washington, USA

JOHN HUNT PUBLISHING

First published by Sixth Books, 2024
Sixth Books is an imprint of John Hunt Publishing Ltd., No. 3 East St., Alresford,
Hampshire SO24 9EE, UK
office@jhpbooks.com
www.johnhuntpublishing.com
www.6th-books.com

For distributor details and how to order please visit the 'Ordering' section on our website.

Text copyright: Alison Grey 2023

ISBN: 978 1 80341 265 8
978 1 80341 266 5 (ebook)
Library of Congress Control Number: 9781803412658

A CIP catalogue record for this book is available from the British Library.

Design: Lapiz Digital Services

UK: Printed and bound by CPI Group (UK) Ltd, Croydon, CR0 4YY
Printed in North America by CPI GPS partners

The author of this book does not dispense medical advice or
prescribe the use of any technique as a form of treatment for
physical, emotional, or medical problems without the advice of a
physician, either directly or indirectly. The intent of the author
is only to offer information of a general nature to help you in
your quest for emotional and spiritual well-being. In the event
you use any of the information in this book for yourself, which is
your constitutional right, the author and the publisher assume no
responsibility for your actions.

We operate a distinctive and ethical publishing philosophy in
all areas of our business, from our global network of authors to
production and worldwide distribution.

# Contents

## Part One

# Welcome

*Nothing can dim the light that shines from within.*
*– Maya Angelou*

Our inner light nestles deeply within our soul and radiates out to the world bringing joy and happiness. When we are aligned with our joy, we are living an authentic life, spreading our positivity to others. Our inner light is our wisdom, our guidance, our truth. It is our gift and our connection to the Divine.

When we are listening to the internal song of our being, we feel connected. Connected to ourselves, others and the universe. We feel the sparks of life bridging and linking together, feeling at peace, in harmony and content.

Listening to my intuition has enabled me to make the most important decisions, helped me meet wonderful people and take some risks along the way which were outside my comfort zone. However, this hasn't always been the case; as a teenager I didn't know who I was, how I fitted in or what my purpose was. I was unaware of my light, my brilliance, my gifts. I felt disconnected at times.

Does this ring true to you? How many of you find it hard to listen to your inner voice, your gut instincts and repeat the same patterns? How many of you are ready to embrace your light and shine brightly?

Our world is a reflection of our inner beliefs. When we are surrounded by people who exude warmth, passion, kindness and love, then we feel it too. It raises our vibration, and we are happy. When those around us are miserable, negative or angry, their energy muddles with our own and can bring us down. What if we could manage this interchangeable roller coaster of

1

emotions, how good would that be? Fear and doubt can hold us back but learning to navigate through them by exploring our limiting beliefs can help us to overcome and tackle them.

As a child I was sensitive and felt emotions deeply, I also had lots of questions so can relate to searching for a more meaningful life, trying to understand who I was and what purpose my life held. During these teenager years, I began reaching out for help from my deceased loved ones, particularly my grandpa. I didn't know where they were, but it seemed natural to communicate with them regardless and felt comforted when answers arrived. How many of you are aware of a deceased loved one helping you out of a tricky situation? Do your children ever say that they feel grandparents looking over them or have a sense of the angelic realms?

During this global pandemic, many parents have contacted me with concerns over their children's mental health and well-being. I am delighted to see how they are trying to support their children to feel safe and protected. My book aims to address this concern with tips and tools for sensitive children to manage their energies (Chapter 24). It aims to encourage parents to use meditation, breathing techniques, crystals and self-care to empower themselves and their children and to listen to their intuition. Listening to your intuition and feeling calm can have a huge positive impact on children's emotions and behaviours.

Every now and again you will have a wobble in your beliefs. It may be a simple casual throw-away remark, a sudden panic or realisation. This is your core belief being tested. Over time, observe these wobbles and setbacks, as I like to call them, they are your teachers too. By observing the patterns in your thinking, your fears and worries, you can find the key to unlock them, face them and push through them. Believe me, you will discover the answers within and it will be easier than you think to conquer them. You will grow from these times. I hope that you will integrate some of the exercises in the book to check into your 'Higher Self' and your angels as part of a daily routine so that you are better equipped to deal with challenging situations.

Throughout our lives we have many teachers and healers, who always seem to appear at the right time. I have been blessed with my spiritual journey to have gained such knowledge through experiences, conversations and extensive reading. I am honoured to be one of your many teachers and would like a chance to help you to have the self-confidence and self-belief to achieve your full potential in life. In my view, however, this can only come about by getting you to understand yourself. Are you ready to commit to your self-discovery and delve deeper into your inner spark and shine brightly?

I am a spiritual teacher, mentor and counsellor. My role is to guide you through your understanding of your soul purpose and help you to understand your true potential. I am here to encourage you to delve beneath the surface, challenge your beliefs, or at the very least, shake them up. My words are a means to a start; it is for you to explore and rummage deeper into your soul for the answers. To understand yourself, believing and engaging with concepts bigger than you had even imagined.

Over the years I've given private readings, I have guided many people of all ages through the ups and downs of their lives. I have encouraged, provided clarity, brought reassurance, hope and healing with the assistance of my guides and their loved ones in Spirit. I take great comfort in the knowledge that people come back regularly and am thankful they refer me to others. Being a spiritual teacher and mentor fills me with pride as I watch my students flourish and grow. I run courses for those of them who want to develop as psychics, mediums or healers, and have included much of my teaching in the book.

During the pandemic and lockdown, many people of all ages were experiencing anxiety and depression because they were terrified of the silence of their inner voice. As a clairvoyant counsellor, teacher and medium, even on Zoom, I've tried to encourage my clients and students to use regular self-care exercises to find the peace within and not allow the atmosphere of fear and panic to allow their fear to hold them back or make them ill. I've been able to support others by giving optimistic messages of hope and reassurance during readings and introducing 'Collective Healing' sessions. These weekly sessions provide distant healing not only for themselves but for their family, friends and pets. We also send out (and still do, as we continue today) healing for the planet and people suffering with the virus and mental health issues. It's powerful work for humanity and really makes a difference.

My hope is that this book will be welcomed by those who wish to focus on their self-care, to help you get in touch with your intuition and to find peace of mind. My wish is for you to discover the significance of finding signs from your loved ones, bringing comfort and guidance in your life. Please use my teaching material, the tools, exercises and my personal experiences to develop your intuitive gifts and understand your soul purpose, allowing the dots to join and your inner light to shine like a star. Let me help you to tune into the language of Spirit.

In writing this book, I have dug deep, baring my soul. I have worked through many challenges and shadows to be where I am today and consider my journey to be ever evolving. Today, I embrace my gifts and wish you to embrace yours too, welcoming your unique journey of discovering where your talents lie and how you can help others for the highest and greatest good of all. But above all to stand confident and assured that there is more to life than what we can see, hear or experience with the human eye. Allow your journey to open your mind to the infinite possibilities and connect you with something special. YOU.

Coincidences are merely Spirit weaving their magic. It is due to Spirit's magical nudges and your conscious decision for change that you have found my book. I am honoured to be your teacher over the following chapters, and hope as you explore the pages, your light grows brighter and nourishes your soul.

Blessings,
Alison

# Chapter 1

# My Awakening

*It is easy to follow your intuition when you have faith and are strong. It is in the darkness, that you need to look within and see your strength. Follow the rhythm of your heart, the whispers of your soul and know that your guides are following alongside you – always.*
*– White Wolf (My animal guide)*

Everybody knows what they fundamentally believe in. It's inside of you, and you live your life according to your beliefs. These beliefs are known to you since birth, creation, but sculpted through life – through infancy, childhood, teenage years and so forth, until they become your core beliefs, what you ultimately stand for. But not everybody feels confident about how they feel or are even connected to their beliefs. This is where I step in. I am a teacher and my role is to guide you in your understanding of yourself.

However, let me start first by saying that we are ALL teachers and we ALL guide others in different ways; we guide others in the exact way that is meant to be, and it is all important. What I will share with you in this book may not be new, it won't necessarily come as a bolt of ingenious revelation, but it will hopefully help and resonate with you, as unbeknown to you, you already understand what I am saying because it forms part of your core belief, a belief that you have already addressed, experienced or witnessed. Reading my words will sit comfortably with you, and although aspects may be new or the slant slightly different, you will understand. My words may prompt questions; this is good as I am here to make you dig beneath your core beliefs, challenge them and shake them up, but I'm also here to help you to grow in your understanding of yourself. As I've said, my words are a means to a start, and it is for you to explore and delve deeper into your own character. There are many teachers and each teacher will present themselves at the right time with the knowledge that there is only perfect timing, in a way that is symbolic to you and you alone.

One teacher alone is not able to teach their student everything; there must be many teachers, many understandings and various perspectives. You will draw upon each understanding, whether read, experienced or observed, and piece together what is right for you and your situation. Over the years I have been lucky enough to have had several fantastic teachers who have each taken me on a wonderful journey of enlightenment, and when I had learnt all they could teach, another teacher appeared. All my teachers (who materialised as mentors, friends, life experiences, books and films) have agreed and contradicted each other, but they have ALL guided my understanding and have developed my core beliefs. It is my role to do the same for you. I am honoured to be one of your many teachers.

You are not the only one on a journey, we ALL are, and we must ALL face our shadow side, the side we run from, bury or ignore as it may be too difficult or we may be ashamed of it. What is a shadow side? Everything in life is balanced. The world, nature, they are all balanced, think of night and day, birth and death, the tides, rich and poor, healthy and unhealthy. We can't feel or express one without the other. Take a happy person who smiles and seems to find life and relationships easy. How can you exude happiness and truly know that state of emotion if you have never experienced sorrow, unhappiness, bad health or loss? Most happy people have reached a compromise; they value what they have rather than chase what they don't have, they are content with themselves. Therefore, they're able to deal with a range of emotions without extremes. And who says that a happy person is happy all the time? We ALL have a shadow side, what we naturally feel when certain situations arise, but we choose to hide from others. Sometimes this is unconscious, but it is what we perceive as being weak or bad. ALL emotions are natural, but it is how we deal with them that matters. For every positive there is a negative, that's life, just the way it is; but in order to be balanced, you need to recognise this. Your shadow side is essential, just like your ego. It is your ego which gets you up in the morning, gives you your passion and pushes you forward; without it you wouldn't get anywhere. However, some people let their ego take charge and that can be destructive. We have a shadow side, let's understand it and use it to our own advantage.

So, what are my core beliefs and what is holding me back? Fear. Fear of being judged. Judged not for what I believe in, I've worked through this, and I'm not fearful of being criticized, as I believe criticism is a necessary teacher and a chance to evolve and deepen our understanding; but a fear that I am unworthy of developing other people. I know I can teach; I have done for over twenty years in different aspects from classroom teaching, SEN, spiritual and running workshops. In these situations, my audience is there to learn; it is when I am being judged on what I say and what I know (not believe). I worry about not getting it right, being understood or having enough knowledge, rather than the material. My confidence therefore becomes the barrier which is holding me back. I am confident, hopefully without being arrogant in most aspects of my life, but standing up in front of adults, scares me for the reason identified: I don't want to be judged.

Fear of failure then is my shadow and I am working through my shadows to become the light. I understand now that writing this book is how I can use the shadows to shine brighter. I am not going to leave anything unturned, I am embracing my gift and baring my whole self. I wish to take you too on this journey of discovering what your gifts are and how you can help others and the planet for the highest and greatest good of all.

Let me start with explaining why I'm writing this book. I was ten when my beautiful paternal grandfather died. The shock was huge and it left a massive hole inside as I had never really experienced death before, not in a person anyway, and I remember sitting at the bottom of the stairs, crying and crying as I realised that I would never see him again. But I did, not in a 'human' way but in my dreams, vivid dreams which touched me so much they had to be real. I also began to have the same recurring dream about my grandfather. On one occasion we were at his house and I sat at the head of the table with my family when unbelievably he sat through me sharing the same time and space with me. We were one and it felt completely normal, yet an odd situation. We connected at this time, close despite time and place. It had taken me many, many years to realise that my grandfather is my spirit guide, and this was his way of showing me. I will discuss more on spirit guides later. How wonderful, to have my grandfather as a guide. I am truly honoured, but he was just the first!

As I was growing up through my teens, I began to experience some odd things happening. I was convinced that there was a figure, I say figure because I didn't know if it was male or female, standing in the corner of my room. I didn't notice it during the day, but when night came, I used to sense it standing there, and although I scared of it, it was because I had no idea what or who it was and I certainly didn't want to see it. I sometimes ran to my parents' bedroom, but they told me I was being silly and to go back to bed. Which I did, hiding under the covers, facing the other way. I didn't feel threatened, but at the same time it unnerved me as I didn't 'know' yet about all this spiritual stuff I was to learn and fast!

Another glimpse to the spiritual world was my connection with my ginger cat, Jerry. He was born under my bed and was my best friend who comforted me when I was upset, felt unheard or lonely. He slept on my pillow, placed his paws around me and nibbled my ear affectionately and was always close. When he died, I used to feel a big compression on the bottom of my bed as if he had jumped up and snuggled down. This comforted me hugely, and although I hazily knew he wasn't there, I could feel him. Once again, I had this huge feeling of connection and I felt totally safe.

Around the age of twelve I remember coming home from school on my own. My sister was supposed to come straight home from school and look after me, but as always, she hung out with her friends and left me home alone. One day I had let myself in, made a cup of tea and a snack and settled down to watch TV. Our family dog Ben lay beside me and we were happy. Moments later I heard someone walking down the stairs, I knew I was alone, so who was this? To add to my fears, my dog sat up and looked inquisitively through the door towards the stairs. No one was there, not physical anyway. I needed no prompting and bolted out of the door and sat in the garden until my sister eventually returned home. I was terrified and confused.

These things I could explain to a degree, but there was something else happening to me which I couldn't. Often as I was falling to sleep, I would have a sensation, the only way I can use to explain it, was my body sinking into my bed whilst I was rising. This sensation scared me as I had absolutely no idea what was happening. I could open my eyes and it would stop, but then resume when I drifted off again. Gradually it began to stop, until, that was, I was pregnant with my first child. I remember this time saying clearly in my mind that I didn't want to die and that I didn't want my baby to die, and as my body (my spirit as I know it to be now) was just emerging out, it stopped and fell back into my body. This was not me dying but my soul going travelling, something I wish would happen again as I am up for the experience and would welcome it wholeheartedly.

The night my Grandpa Les died I had an unforgettable dream. I was in church visiting a confessional box. I remember it clearly, it was wooden and had intricate carvings on it, and as I approached it and went inside my grandpa was sitting behind the screen. He was saying goodbye and I knew instantly that he had died. That is the odd thing about Spirit dreams, you know they are a dream, yet you know they are real, and you feel the emotion so deeply. After he had said goodbye to me, he asked if all my cousins would enter the confessional box, and one by one, he said goodbye to them all. I woke the next morning to the heartbreaking news of my grandpa's death.

In the following weeks, my sadness was up and down. I hated the thought of never being able to see, talk or cuddle my grandpa in the same way again, yet I instinctively knew he was safe and in Heaven (wherever that was). It was my nan who I felt my heart break for, she missed my grandpa, who she met at only 16 years old, desperately. They had never been apart. It was around this time that I started to write poetry, and not ordinary poetry. I loved writing and reading but never considered myself an eighteen-year-old poet, however, it just seemed to flow from my pen, and it was mainly written with words that I wouldn't usually speak. I wrote about abstract things which seemed to make sense of my grief and I knew that the poems, well two anyway, were for my nan. She apparently loved them and placed the poems in frames, hanging them in her home. I now know this to be channelling from spirit, a method used to write something which isn't from you but from somebody in the spirit world (my grandpa in this case) for somebody else. It is like writing in a light trance; you know you are doing it but you don't really know what you are writing, it just comes into your mind and you write, type, sing or speak.

Another strange, but not scary experience I was getting was frequent light flickering, my music suddenly being turned on/off and the volume being tampered with. I remember being in the shower, I was the only person in the house as everyone was at work (I was a student so didn't need to be in lectures until the afternoon). I had been listening to music but had turned it off as I was going to the shower, however, with my hair covered in shampoo, my stereo suddenly came on and the music was turned up so loud that I had to get out of the shower in order to turn it down. It was my grandpa letting me know he was there to say, "Hello." This was an example of many spooky things which happened to me over time.

I was twenty years old when I had my first psychic reading. It was just after I had split from my boyfriend of four years. I didn't even know you could have a psychic reading, didn't really know what it was apart from someone telling me what my future will hold. I was amazed, knocked off my seat and totally hooked from my first-ever reading with the delightful Mrs Loveridge.

How did she know these things about me? How could she read my character or know how I have been feeling? How was she able to see into the future, at what was likely to become my destiny? I needed to know. I also needed to know what the cards she was using were called. I was amazed that she could determine truth from pictures and pictures which didn't reveal much. As we drove home, I knew that I was going to get myself some of those cards! And I did. Well, according to the whispers I heard, you are not meant to buy your own cards but to have them given to you. That was easy to figure out. I bought some for my mum who liked them but didn't feel drawn to them, so she gave them to me. Perfect. I now owned a set of Tarot cards – the first of many, many decks as I later decided that I didn't believe old wives' tales and bought my own.

I instantly started shuffling the deck, dealing card after card and absorbing the images in front of me. Unsure what they meant, I sourced the guidebook, and after a while, the tarot became like weaving stories and I loved it. I was amazed at how much the pictures could say, they can talk, and soon, I was reading for my family and friends. But that wasn't the only thing that was developing. I began to see images and feel things.

As a child, I could always sense people's emotions. I knew when they were upset, cross or not telling the truth. My tummy would tell me, and I was very perceptive picking up body language. I'm not saying I knew what they had done or what they were thinking. I could just tell that what they were telling me wasn't true. A knowing, particularly helpful later in life with boyfriends, good and bad. In fact, the night I met my now husband, I just knew we were going to marry one day, he was the one.

Being pregnant stirred up my sensitive side, my senses became extra heightened and I started to get my 'funny feelings' of floating again. I would lie in bed at night and feel myself rising, pushing up to the top of my body as if I was going to pop out and fly free. I was always able to stop myself but this time, eight-and-a-half months pregnant, it scared me as I thought, what if I died? I remember sending up a prayer pleading not to die and taking my unborn child with me. I obviously didn't and I've only had that experience a few times since. I now know that this weird sensation is called astral travelling and I'd love to experience it again, this time coming out of my body properly. I will have to wait and see if that is meant for me.

After my second son was born, images repetitively flashed into my mind. I could see flashes of people I knew were in the spirit world and images of things that connected to them. One example was of my Grandpa Les which was closely followed by a navy ship. I knew it was all connected and understood that these were messages, but apart from that, I had no idea what was going on. After a few months, I decided to go and see a medium whom I had read an article about in a magazine and worked not far from me in Waltham Abbey.

As I was having my reading, the lady picked up on my spiritual gifts, and said I could and should develop them further. In fact, she was running a development course that was due to start, however, I had a small baby and a two-year-old. It wasn't possible for me at this time, so I left it. The images and dreams continued as did my passion on all things spiritual, but I didn't consider developing it further.

# Chapter 2

# My Next Steps

When I was 33, I started going to a healing group with my aunt. What I didn't know then, but I do know now, is that 33 is the Christ number, the age at which Jesus stepped into his spiritual self and I feel this too was my journey, where I finally understood that my life was important. Not just because I was a mother and a teacher, but because I had another role to play and a mission to fulfil. I just wasn't clear about what that was yet.

I loved the weekly healing circle; not only did I meet some wonderful like-minded people with my aunt, but I also got to receive healing. Each week we would focus on a different type of healing, however, at this stage it was only Spiritual healing. Feeling the amazing warmth and energy flowing through my body was marvellous and it really helped to relax me. It was where I was also introduced to meditation. I found that I could really switch off my busy mind, and visualisation came easily to me. Exploring the wonderful sounds and sights of nature catapulted me to another level of consciousness, it was addictive. When Jo, one of the leaders, asked if I wanted to write my own, I recoiled in horror. I never could imagine that my words could have such a profound effect on somebody's state of mind and body – little did I realise then that I'd be writing many, many guided meditations for all ages.

To be honest, although I loved receiving healing, I was unsure whether I was gifted to give it to others. I had never imagined this before but as I held my hands over a lady's head, I could feel the heat and a pounding sensation building up within them. Amazed when the lady commented on how strong the energy was, she could feel it. I hovered my hands around the other chakras and then scanned the aura for areas in need of healing. One time, I was giving spiritual healing to a lady when I had a sensation of being blocked around the head. From there, I felt a whoosh of energy speed through her to her feet. I also heard, "Keep calm." Afterward, the lady confirmed that she was moving to a new house which was stressing her and that she had recently hurt her ankle.

Over the coming months, I realised that I could see a beautiful peacock-blue light emerging from my hands when I gave healing and that my hands came to life, guiding me to places of injury or tension. My confidence grew as I began to feel changes in the energy, for example sometimes my hands felt hot when there was inflammation, other times they would go freezing cold. The members of the group could feel this change too, apparently it is common, but I had no prior experience of this up till now. I could also sense the energy of a person, whether their chakras were too open or indeed closed. I loved this! The more I spent with this healing group, the more talk of other healing filled my ears, sparking my interest further. I was introduced to Reiki and Rahanni, crystal, colour and sound healing, all of which brought such healing to others.

I soon found myself as a Reiki Master and a Rahanni teacher, a Reiki drum practitioner, and also I studied a diploma in crystal healing and Atlantean healing, but this took years and I feel I was brought each healing modality when it was my soul's purpose to hold their energies within my aura. Trance healing became one of my favourites, I would love both being the trance healer and the battery – this is where the healers use your energy as a battery to hold the healing energy high for guides to step into and blend with their medium to give intense healing. When the guides blend with the medium, transfiguration takes place and you can see subtle changes in the medium's face or posture take shape. This experience is simply amazing and special. One session, I was standing behind a lady when I suddenly became aware of a huge brown bear and felt it was protecting her.

When we finished, I asked the lady if this meant anything to her and she confirmed her spiritual animal was indeed 'Remus' the bear.

As time passed, I found that I looked forward to the healing circle more and more. My aunt and I were totally inspired by all the spiritual experiences and talk, I couldn't get enough of it and we naturally gravitated towards a spiritual circle. Healing was well and truly ingrained in me and was my natural way of living, but now it was my time to explore my psychic and mediumship gifts.

I was extremely nervous sitting in my first circle, I had no idea what it was going to be like and was apprehensive about the type of people that attended. I was so glad my aunt was also joining with me. As I sat down, within a circle of chairs, it dawned on me that there were about twenty other people. Luckily, all normal and friendly. One of my first memories came halfway through that very first session. The lady running it suddenly turned to me and asked me to stand up and connect with spirit. I'd been happily sitting in the wonder energy of spirit and watching how others could stand up, link in and identify loved ones through their appearance, characteristics and memories before giving a message. Now it was my turn and I had no idea how to do it, so I refused, point-blank refused, as did my aunt. I totally wasn't ready, even though this was exactly why I was there. My nervousness kicked in and I just wanted everyone to stop looking at me. Afterwards, at the end, this lovely gentle teacher turned to my aunt and me and said, "Next time I ask you to stand, I expect you to get up." Harsh, but right and I came back the next week and did just that.

There were two teachers that day, the lady who owned the centre whom I had had a reading from and suggested I join, and the softer lady who spoke so direct to me. To say I was petrified was an understatement. I felt like I was back in my teens in a maths lesson where a scary teacher used to pick on me the whole time expecting me to know the answers to difficult sums.

With the blood draining from me and my heart pounding, I rose and took my position with around twenty pairs of eyes staring at me.

I took a couple of deep breaths, and out of nowhere I could see images tumbling into my mind. I could see clearly and in colour. I also felt and understood things, however, I felt I was making it all up. Being encouraged to share what I was experiencing I started to speak. I could see my uncle in my mind and described him, he was alive and well, but I came to realise that this is how spirit can help you identify people in the spirit world. As I continued to describe his height, clothes and personality I was amazed to see that somebody could take my information. My teacher pressed me further and I started to see events unfolding. Objects to start with and then places, all of which could be understood. Wow, I wasn't making it up after all!

As the months passed, one thing kept coming up for me: why could I see all these things, sense and know them but I couldn't see and hear spirit like everyone said they could? It really baffled me. It was then it was explained to me that actually all these mediums weren't seeing spirit like they were 'real' people and they weren't hearing them in the spirit's voice, they were using their 'clairs', their extrasensory senses of clairvoyance, clairsentience and clairaudience. With this knowledge I began to relax into my development, and my own senses deepened. I really enjoyed the psychic exercises of psychometry, reading tarot, colours, people's energy and, reading anything and everything – even tissues! (Clean ones of course.)

Around two years in, I was offered a mentorship with my now friends. There were two groups, but I was to be in the second group as my connection with spirit came slowly. With a promise to work hard and trust more (this had always been my problem) it was agreed, and I joined an amazing group of other developing mediums. We would meet every month for a whole weekend for six months and I loved every moment, well except the platform part where I had to demonstrate my mediumship. The nervousness just kept coming even though I was developing my links and my evidence was more accurate. I remember one day my teacher began knocking the wall as I was working and said, "This is the sound of your guides banging their heads on a brick wall." My lesson was to trust, to believe what I was getting, and I worked hard to say what I got without questioning. This took time and I still sometimes question my evidence today, but the difference is that I totally believe and ultimately trust in spirit. In fact, I now know that if my information can't be understood it is because of me, my energy and my interpretation. Spirit wants us to help, they will not give us wrong information, they do not wish for us to fall flat on our faces, they want to communicate. It is our job as a medium to listen.

Although I spent years sitting in circles and partook in three intense mentorship programmes, taking workshops and developing my interest in healing and past life regression and reading countless books, I believe that I am still learning today. I learn from my guides, sitting with them and listening, paying attention to the signs they and the angels send me. I also learn from my 1:1 private reading and through teaching my circle. There is always more to learn and grow. Life brings experiences, highs and lows – these are all our teachers. Sitting regularly in a circle can really boost your mediumship as it sends out the signal to the Spirit World that you are serious about connecting. It raises your vibration, and with like-minded friends, you can support, and problem solve. A circle isn't just about developing, it's fine-tuning and keeping you in the energy of spirit. Some people feel that they have reached the point where they can work on their own and are regularly giving readings, perhaps professionally and they no longer can learn from others, but

I beg to differ. I may not sit in a circle but I run one and have either sat or run circles since I began this journey; as I said earlier, I too learn through my students and my teaching pushes my boundaries with the Spirit World and I will continue to teach for as long as Spirit want me to.

My circle has the most wonderful group of mediums. When I first started out I had only three people, including my aunt. Each Tuesday we would sit in a cold, dimly-lit shed at the back of a garden centre, but it didn't matter to us as we were communicating with spirit and developing. After some time, the little place was sold, and I moved our circle to a children's pottery shop which had amazing energy and a kettle for our tea and biscuits. Through word of mouth we expanded and shared many messages from our loved ones, however, once again the shop was sold, and I was lucky enough to find a spiritual shop with a room to hire. This was brilliant as the owner had already run a circle and I was able to take over, merging mine with hers. For a while we built up the energy in the shop, but alas, this too shut down. I was beginning to think that everything was against me when a beautiful friend and member of my group suggested that we use her flat, both in fact as she also moved. I felt happy and comfortable teaching and loved watching the mediums grow in a safe environment. Every member of my circle encouraged and supported each other, a far cry from some of the circles I sat in which could become rooms of egos at times. I feel because of the friendship, trust and love we became (and still are today) close friends. Circle is so important to me that when I found out I was pregnant with my fourth boy, I hardly took any time off and returned with him in arms, breastfeeding whilst I taught. Not many mediums could say they had been taught in such an environment, but this is testament to my students/friends. Again, through word of mouth, we continued to expand, having now up to twenty members (they don't all come at once, but

I do have the regulars which turn up each week). I felt honoured that they trusted my teaching and I was, and still am, so excited to see them grow in their own development. They are amazing!

Suddenly, as I arrived at this point in my life, everything changed. With just over a year since my fourth son was born, my dad died. My dad was my rock; alongside my mum, together they were always there for me. Dad was the typical protective father, the man who instilled my values and helped the family with any job that needed doing. He was a wonderful father and grandfather; his sudden death shocked us all. I remember when I received the call from Mum that he had had a car accident and was being taken to hospital. I knew deep down within my soul it was serious, yet I begged my angels to help and not let him die. I mean really begged and I kept begging all the way to the hospital. It was when I reached High Barnet and was stopped by a red traffic light that I paused and felt my dad sitting next to me in the car. I looked at the clock for some reason and it read 14.44. In that moment, I only felt how odd it was, but in reality, I now know that 444 is an angel number to reassure us that an army of angels are surrounding us. He had passed. I looked out the window, whilst willing the lights to change, and saw the estate agent's 'Martyn Gerard', my dad's first name spelt exactly as he did, with a 'y'. I knew, yet knew, he had passed to spirit, and I was a mess. This couldn't be happening and not to my dad. I hadn't experienced emotion and sadness like this before, it ripped my whole world.

As the months passed, I felt my dad around me constantly which was a huge comfort. It still is and I have him to thank for so many positive changes. For example, I know that he was instrumental in moving my growing circle to my mum's house. I feel that not only has he deepened my mediumship, but he also created an opportunity for Mum and me to regularly be with each other. It brought my mum and me even closer as I had moved to Oxfordshire and couldn't always come down to see her as my other boys were in school. Now I came down every other week to see her and run my circle. As she looks after my smallest, I run my circle and give readings. My dad's presence is so strong at my mum's and he brings the most wonderful energy. None of this would have come about if Dad was still alive, but from the other side, he guided me. Sometimes we would use another member of the circle's house and it seemed that whatever obstacles were put in place, together we showed up to spirit to learn. My students were unfazed with the changes and we met regardless. In fact, as I write this, I teach my circle every Tuesday over Zoom! Nothing will get in our way. I even run a second successful and equally friendly and supportive circle in Chipping Norton.

I am so grateful for the opportunity to work with spirit and thankful that my students/friends trust me and will follow me wherever, but I also know that I am not the only one holding the group together, they are the glue and their bond is strong. They believe in each other, and as I have said already, are supportive and encouraging. The most perfect mediums, doing spiritualism proud.

# Chapter 3

# Guides

Guides are wonderful spiritual beings who join us for our ride through life. There are six different types of guides from Archangels, Guardian Angels, Spirit Guides, Loved Ones, Spirit Animals and Helper Guides.

In this chapter, I want to introduce you to Spirit Guides and Animal Guides. Spirit Guides take the form of people, they are wise beings who have reached and earned the right to guide others through their life journey. Their knowledge and understanding of our soul mission means they can send us signs to steer us through the most difficult situations and help to keep us on our soul path so that we learn our lessons, meet the people we need to meet and be in the right place at the right time, for our souls to grow.

Spirit Guides, unlike angels, have had previous incarnations here on Earth. They have walked their own path and possibly have joined us along a previous path that we have shared together. They are present at the 'Planning Stages' as we prepare to incarnate (I will touch on this topic later in the book) and know the overall map of our life. As they are not bound to the 'Free Will' law, they can step in and advise us when we need help, without us having to ask. It is, in my opinion, great practice to graciously invite them to help us and show respect for their support by regularly giving gratitude and thanks.

It is common that we can have several Spirit Guides. Some will be close throughout our entire lifetime; others may come and grace our time for a specific reason or situation. You will usually have one main guide, who walks alongside you, but because you are a special soul, there may be many guides who have chosen to offer their unique gifts to you, bringing an abundance of different qualities and lessons. These may include animal guides so you can tap into their 'animal' qualities like the strength and courage of a lion, or to see the higher perspective of an eagle. Feeling a strong connection with your guides is normal, you have spent many lifetimes together! Guides are like your family members or best friends who readily offer their support.

I have been asked many times, "Do our guides only work with us?" "Are they exclusive to us?"

No is the short answer. Some are, but generally they are teachers for many others too, but this by no means reduces their love, respect and quality of their guidance.

Meditation is a marvellous way to meet your spirit guides. In this altered state, your conscious mind cannot 'pop' ideas into your head of fancy Kings, Queens or important people. In fact, our guides are general ordinary people who we have walked side-by-side with in previous lives. As I said previously, our guides are very normal and can have very normal names.

One time I set my intention to meet my spirit guide, and as he began to blend with me, I could see a young monk or friar with a beautiful, peaceful face. I knew he was from Italy and I heard the name "Francis" and "Roberto". Over the next couple of days, all I could see were references to monks, Italy and then something prompted me to google Francis, Italy and monks. I was astonished when I found that the Franciscan monks were members of the Roman Catholic religion, founded by Saint Francis of Assisi and the most prominent group is that of the 'Order of Friars Minor', commonly known as the 'Franciscan'. I also kept seeing the name Rob or Robert, so I now understand this as my Guide's name, and as he draws close to me my ear goes cold inside and I have a wave of comfort, that I'm most grateful for.

Further confirmation happened the next day when my husband put on the radio and the DJ was called Roberto who happened to introduce a winning trip to Italy. Wondering where I was going to get another third monk confirmation, I turned my head and my eyes focused on a book on my shelf, *The Monk Who Sold His Ferrari* by Robin Sharma. I am just so in awe of the spirit world and how it can bring messages and signals to us.

To give you an understanding of the wide spectrum and quantity of guides, I will briefly introduce my guides to you.

After my Reiki 111 Attunement, I had a beautiful vision of a stunning dragon with the most powerful sense of protection and strength. Over the coming days, I saw many images of dragons, they were literally everywhere.

Trance Guide – I have a hooded man who carried a staff. I knew he was Chinese when an image of Gismo popped into my mind and saw a long pointy beard. With the vision, I experienced an amazingly strong energy flowing down my head, through my neck. Again, as always, needing confirmation, I asked them to show me some signs. I received two references to China, more dragon references and a child advert for 'Ninja Warriors' with the little sensei figure looking exactly as I had seen him. I have since understood that Tibet is relevant to me and my guide so believe we shared a lifetime together there.

My Rahanni guide is a Tibetan monk, he was very proud of his orange robes. He is an old man, small with worn hands. He brings a beautiful and peaceful energy with him. I have to admit that I don't know their names. I was told names are not important which I've accepted, however, when healing, I call upon both my sensei and Tibetan monk and feel their hands placed upon my back as if someone were placing their palms flat. The sensation is cool and I'm grateful when they appear, knowing they are strengthening and accelerating my healing. I do, however, cheekily call them Bill and Ben – my healing men! They come, so I don't think they mind.

Another guide I wish to share with you is Daybreak; he is a Cherokee medicine man and helps me with all aspects of my spiritual work. Daybreak popped into my meditation, and when I asked for a name, I saw a wonderful image of Dawn – the break of day. The name was spectacularly confirmed for me when I walked into a supermarket to a children's book display with a massive banner on which read 'Day-Break', talk about in your face. The sign was put there for me to read and being someone who works with children and having written a children's book, I think that was very clever. Thank you.

White Wolf is my special animal guide, my spiritual teacher and guide. I often just see his yellow eyes looking at me, but the days after I first met him, I saw wolf poems at school, *Peter and the Wolf* in the library and images of wolves shown to me by a girl in my class. I also have other marvellous guides, all who help me in different ways, but connect regularly and bring me support, strength, understanding, knowledge and creative ideas.

My other guides which I work closely with are:

Tomahawk – Secret Knowledge and healing

Charlie – He introduced himself in knight's armour with an England flag. He showed me the round table of King Arthur, so I know this is relevant. I have since had a past life regression where I was a medicine lady in Avalon times.

Seraphina and Sunrise – Unicorn guides

Sparky and Star – Dragon guides

Targo – Atlantean guide

Odin (also known as Merlin) – Alchemy and runes

Shona – Her face pops right into mine as if she is reading me. She has only appeared a handful of times, but she is checking me out and will become stronger when the time is right.

Isis – The beautiful black panther with green eyes

Ozzy the Osprey – Clairvoyance. I thought Ozzy was an eagle, however, I stand corrected when he showed me the box of a wallet I gave to my husband one Christmas, it was from the company of Osprey.

Any time I need advice or reassurance, I sit in the power for communication with my guides. This is a perfect way to link in with your guides and allow them to give you the messages you need to receive. I will either see or sense my guides, and their communication comes in many different forms. Sometimes they show me visions, other times it comes as animals, images, or symbols. It is important to simply observe, because if you try to figure it all out during your meditation that will stop the flow of communication, switch your conscious mind back on to full alert and you may miss the next piece of vital information. Never mind if you fall asleep either (I often do – I have a busy life), you will remember all you need to remember and the rest will be given to you at soul level so it is in your energy for retrieval when it is needed. Although I try to sit with spirit regularly, and advise you to do so, my guides know I am busy, so pop in when I'm calm or doing something mundane or something I can do with my eyes closed – like cooking or driving (not really closed). Either way, if they have a message for you, they will bring it to you. Remember, guides include the angelic realms too and the Ascended Masters, so watch out for them.

Through my guidance, listening closely to the whispers, I went on to start my own healing and spiritual circles; teaching, healing, children and working for the Spirit World are my soul's purpose, what I am here to do in this incarnation and I am truly grateful, blessed and honoured to do so. At first, I combined my day job, a special needs teacher, with my 'spooky' side as I like to call it. I held my spiritual circle on a Tuesday evening and my healing circle during a Thursday morning when the boys were at school. I also began to give 1:1 readings, my clients coming through word of mouth. Calmer Kids was slowly taking shape and my wonderful husband and parents were always on hand to help me with childcare. I studied past life regression – such a fascinating and amazing healing tool, and also incorporated that into my life. It wasn't until I had my fourth son and our house became too small, that we needed to move. This fortuitous time enabled me to give up teaching in schools and really focus on my spiritual work and develop Calmer Kids into the success it is today.

When I tell people that everything happens for a reason, it does, and my life with all its ups and downs, chance meetings and coincidences has led me onto my true path. My trust in the Spirit World is so vast, that I know they have my future planned too, and with my guides, intuition, the angels and family and friends, I look forward to watching it continue to unfold. My wish is to help as many people and children as I possibly can, spreading healing, proving the existence of the Spirit World, reuniting passed souls with their loved ones and teaching everything I have been taught, shown and experienced. I am not the kind of teacher to tell you what is right or wrong, that is your job to understand. I was guided by my loved ones, guides, angels and teachers, you will be too.

Below are some ways which you can meet and connect with your Spirit Guide.

- Guided meditation
- Meditation
- Dreams
- Journaling
- Inner Knowledge
- Signs – ask, then wait for them to appear (read the next chapter for the types of signs you may receive)

One final note, don't get too hung up by names. Most guides are not really interested in their form or name. You will undoubtably receive images of them to start with so your human brain can understand them, but after recognising how they feel when they are present, the guides normally connect with you via clairsentience or claircognizance (feeling and sensing them). This is a comforting sign; it means your relationship with your guides has evolved as this way of working is faster. It means you have fully accepted trust and believe in their guidance.

# Chapter 4

# Signs from Spirit

I haven't just had signs from guides, I have received signs from my loved ones too, and these are the most precious gifts you could ask for as they are messages of love, comfort and guidance. I have been aware of the signs of spirit since I was little. I always found it strange when these synchronicities appeared, and I always smiled and gave thanks. Such signs would sometimes make me shiver or go 'goosy'. I have mentioned already the time my grandpa connected with me to make me aware he would be taking my nan soon, and when he turned my music up so high, I had to get out of the shower. However, over my many years I have received so many signs which have either been 'Hellos' or 'guidance'. My grandpas both visit me and my family via robins in the garden and my nan leaves pennies or shiny 5p's in unusual places. I find they turn up around birthdays or the date they went home to Heaven. They come when I'm feeling fed up or sad, but on one occasion I found a penny under my bottom on the car seat when I was looking at primary schools for my eldest son. I knew for a fact it wasn't there when I got into the car and I didn't see it when I got out, but when I returned it was shining bright, you couldn't miss it. The meeting with the head hadn't gone well. The school I was visiting was a great sought-after school, but the headteacher kept me waiting ages and didn't sell her school, giving me an odd feeling. I returned to the car and saw the penny as clear as can be on my seat. Still confused, I am a sceptic who questions everything, I opened the boot of my car (I can't remember why now) but a bag of old stuff that my mum had wanted me to take from her house, but I didn't know where to put so had left in the boot, had opened and the contents spilled out. I noticed a gold-plated desk calendar which was my Grandpa Jack's had fallen out, and as I picked it up, I saw the date of my twenty-week maternity scan which was coming up. I knew instantly he was with me and would guide me to the right school. A month later, I was chatting to a lady who told me about another school, an Ofsted Outstanding school that wasn't on my radar. I was bowled over when I visited, so much so that I felt I could teach there myself, and although we were not Christian, had no special needs or siblings and it was slightly out of my catchment area, my eldest won a place there. This was to be a pattern with all my children's nurseries, primary and secondary schools. All Outstanding and all difficult to get into. My grandpa was an intelligent man and looks after my children's education. In fact, I was told recently by one of my students as she gave me a message from my grandpa that he looks after my little one and that each of my boys is looked after by a spirit member of my family. When I linked in and asked them, I was shown that my 12-year-old has my nan looking after him, he looks just like her and has similar traits, my dad looks after my 14-year-old and 6-year-old, whilst my eldest is looked after by my mother-in-law. How special is that, how lucky are they?

When my second child was born, I would wake up in the middle of the night to feed him. It would be pitch-black outside, and the windows shut, not a soul on the streets or in their gardens. I recall vividly on numerous occasions the strong recognisable smell of smoke and knew instantly that my Grandpa Les was around. He was a heavy smoker, the only one in the family at that time who had passed to the spirit world, and I'd get a sense of love surrounding me. Knowing he was around brought me comfort, he would have loved great-grandchildren. My only sorrow was that he never got to see them in his lifetime, although I know he would argue that he gets to see all his great-grandchildren all of the time, whenever he wishes.

Feathers are another way that our loved ones, spirit and angels let us know they are around and I have found thousands of them in unusual places and they always show up when

I need an answer, am feeling low or remembering a special occasion like a birthday. I was teaching some students in my development circle and we were halfway through the evening when Lesley our host got up to make us tea and we had a little toilet break. When I came back to my seat, a perfect white feather was perched delicately on top of my notepad. No one had gone outside, the blinds and windows were shut and seeing as though Lesley lived in a one-bedroom flat on the first floor, it simply couldn't have wafted in. I took that as a sign that we were in the company of spirit and that they were supporting the learning which was taking place. We were all amazed and all felt honoured to receive such a sign.

Robins frequently come to visit, as I have already mentioned. I used to believe them to be the spirit of both my grandpas, but lately my dad too. Some may say they are birds in nature and would argue that they are around naturally, being close as they are territorial birds, but when you receive robins as a sign, you definitely know because they come with the most amazing feeling of love and warmth. My sister gifted me and my mum with a hanging robin last Christmas, but I haven't put him away, I love the knowledge that my dad is around me in my kitchen. It is wildly known that robins with their glowing redbreasts are signs of our loved ones, although they can take form in any bird. My mother-in-law is a beautiful wagtail who hops around our garden, looking into our house, trying to catch our eye. One of my guides who helps me develop my clairvoyance, amongst other spiritual gifts, is an Osprey as I mentioned earlier; when I see them flying above or I see an image of one, then I know he is close by. It is the same with wolves and black panthers.

My wonderful nan sends pennies, they are everywhere including in the seal of my washing machine. Again, this can happen if you carry money in your pockets, but I don't, and we tease my husband about never carrying cash saying he is like 'The Queen'. So how is finding a 5p in the washing machine a sign? It is the timing and thoughts in my mind at that specific time which makes finding pennies special. They do appear from nowhere, literally, trust me. If you haven't received a penny from a special person in spirit, ask them to send you one. You will believe it then, honestly. My nan, not wanting to be the same as everyone else, has begun to send shiny 5p's. I can hear her in my mind, saying everyone sends pennies, I will send you something else and she does, birthdays, Christmas, anniversaries and sometimes just to say hello. Remember, apart from them being found in unusual places, they can turn up and appear out of the blue. I often find them on the seat I was sitting on or on the table next to me or in my underwear drawer, when they weren't there a second ago. I find those times, magical.

Spirit finds it easy to play with electrical and metal things, it seems easy for them to do. A few years back I realised that my nan's wedding ring was missing. It was always in my jewellery box, but I couldn't find it. It was odd because my aunt had also lost one of my nan's rings, hers had been missing for ages though. I was really upset, I remember, as it was her first wedding ring my grandpa had bought her; it was a simple thin gold band (he later bought her a more expensive one) but this ring to me was far more valuable in terms of sentimental value. I didn't tell anyone; I was annoyed at myself for misplacing it and hoped I would find it. A few weeks went past and I was going camping with my husband and boys. I had bought a packet of new knickers and one morning while packing my wash bag and clothes, I reached for some folded knickers (they had already been opened because I had worn several pairs), when something fell out and landed on my lap. It was my nan's ring! Apart from being elated and grateful, I was stunned and shocked. My nan had taken the ring and returned it to me in the most unexpected way. A real sign she is around, along with the song *Over the Rainbow* which I heard not long afterwards, and a link to my nan's memory.

Funnily enough, around a similar time, my aunt was babysitting for her granddaughters at my cousin's. The next morning, his girlfriend rang my aunt to ask if she had lost her ring as she found one in the sofa. My aunt checked her fingers, no ring was missing but asked her to describe it. Sure enough, it was my nan's ring, the exact one she had lost. Like me, the ring had been taken and returned in a completely different place. I think my nan likes to prove a point about the spirit world. It's like she is saying, "I won't just take an object and then give it back, I will move it miles away and return it in spectacular fashion. Then you will believe I'm around still." My nan always did like to stand out and receive special attention. You see they take their personalities with them to the other side!

**Other signs you may encounter are:**

- Feathers
- Street names
- Names of houses
- Birds
- Rainbows and clouds
- Music – song titles, a special song, lyrics
- Butterflies, dragonflies
- Insects or animals
- Number sequences
- Recurring times e.g. time of death or birth
- A book may fall off the shelf, be placed upside down etc
- Newspaper articles
- Interview or YouTube video with a special meaning
- Smells – smoke, perfume, familiar scent
- Dreams

I can't say I fully understand the physics surrounding the realms of time and space or how they can move objects, however,

I know it is about 'altering energy', and Spirit are able to do so in order to manipulate objects.

Spirit understand that life can be challenging, they are also aware of our grief, so once they have passed, they send us signs to let us know they are still around us. Believe me when I say the signs will always come, with Divine timing.

# Chapter 5

# The Angelic Realm

*Your spiritual journey is reflected in you. Be gracious and true.*
*I will accompany you over the bridge of light on your ascension*
*path. My golden orange light is your guide. My gift to you is*
*spiritual wisdom.*
*– Archangel Metatron*

I have always believed in angels, but I had never seen or felt one
until I started this magical journey and began opening up. You
see, angels are bound by free will, they are only able to grace us
with their presence or intervene if we ask them, unless acting
out of Universal Law of Fate. This means if we are in danger,
yet it is not our time to die, then they will step in and save us.
There have been many hundreds and thousand of stories which
witness this.

Angels are messengers of God, healers and protectors.
They are unconditional love and here for everyone, not just
spiritual people who regularly connect with them. Angels are
drawing ever closer to us because many of us are opening up to
spirituality and ascending at this time, and the angelic realm is
helping us to do this. In fact, you don't have to believe in them
for them to be there and help you, another example of their
unconditional love.

Angels are pure beings of Divine light bringing love into our
lives, helping us every day from our mundane chores to our life
missions. They help us behind the scenes when we need them
most, in times of trouble, grief, pain or loss of direction. Angels
have never been human, they have never walked on Earth as
we do. They are non-denominational, have both masculine and
feminine energy, and to some, like me, they come as flashes

of coloured lights. I can feel their wings, I can melt into their arms and blend with their energy but I've never seen an angel standing in front of me with wings outstretched as they do in films, books or to some lucky ones. You may experience them differently. It is my belief that you see what you want to see. If you need to believe in angels, then you may 'see' them. I trust they are around, and being clairsentient, I feel and absorb their energies and 'hear' their wisdom and nudgings.

Angels communicate with us subtly, they will gently nudge us, send us signs through feathers or numbers, or will make sure the things we need to know, read or go are placed right under our noses. Have you ever heard a certain song or lyric which resonates with you at a particular moment in time? Or has a particular book fallen off the shelf in front of you or been recommended several times to you before it has been reviewed in a magazine or placed right in front of you in a public place? Well this is the silent work of the magnificent angels.

## The Archangels

Archangels are beings of light. They are God's messengers and have been around since time began. All angels are androgynous meaning they have both masculine and feminine energies which are perfectly balanced and vibrate with a high energy. They are unconditional love which they radiate with abundance. Archangels carry our thoughts and prayers to God, and help guide, protect and assist us in our everyday life. These magnificent beings of light govern our chakras and help us to ascend. Each Archangel carries specific gifts that we can call upon readily, they are just waiting for us to ask.

There are many Archangels and each of them has a twin flame, however, I am only going to mention the Angels that I have come across during my journey and will try to capture their wonderful energies in words, or at least how they make me feel emotionally.

An important note to remember, angels are energy, they have sparks of The Divine and can work, under Grace, for all. They are multidimensional and can be in many places at the same time, so please don't feel that because someone else is calling upon them, they will not come to you. They most certainly will, just ask. There are no limits to how many people they can help at any one time, they are blessed with unlimited time and energy. Gold is the colour of angelic vibration so surrounding yourself in a bubble of shimmering gold will help raise your vibration and allow the angels to connect and blend with your energy.

## Meet the Archangels

### Archangel Ariel

'Lion or lioness of God'. Ariel is involved with healing and protecting nature, animals, including fish and birds. He has a wonderfully gentle energy and I feel very safe when he is around. He works with people who are involved with animals and those who teach.

### Archangel Azrael

'Whom God helps'. Azrael's role is to help people cross over to heaven at the time of physical death. He lovingly comforts people prior to their physical death, ensuring there is no suffering, then helps them once they arrive on the other side.

### Archangel Chamuel

'He who sees God', Archangel Chamuel links in with our heart centres. He brings comfort, unconditional love, tolerance and protection. Archangel Chamuel is gentle, kind, loving and helps us with forgiveness. Working with your heart centre brings Archangel Chamuel close, and when in his presence there is an amazing glow and sense of deep peace. Our hearts hold 33 petals of Christ energy, working with Archangel Chamuel helps us to open them. I love asking Archangel Chamuel to come close when I am focusing on my heart centre and working with children and adults who need to open to love and forgiveness.

## Archangel Christiel

I see Archangel Christiel as a moon. She brings in the Christ light through her pearl white light. Archangel Christiel helps us to connect with the angelic realm, the spiritual kingdom. Her gentle yet powerful divine feminine energy makes her a wonderful Archangel to connect with.

## Archangel Mallory

Archangel Mallory is the twin flame and Divine Feminine of Archangel Christiel. She is a burgundy colour, which combines beautifully the gold light of Christ for wisdom and red for action when you need to get going on a task. She is the Keeper of Ancient Wisdom and connects with your Causal chakra. I love to call upon Archangel Mallory to help me understand who I am to encourage me, with strength, to complete my soul purpose.

## Archangel Gabriel

'God is my strength'. He is the angel of child conception, including working with parents who wish to adopt. Archangel Gabriel helps us with loving communication. He over-lights our joy, helping us to see with more clarity, and brings hope. Archangel Gabriel is a mighty powerful Archangel and I call upon him regularly for many reasons. He feels strong, knowledgeable and dependable with a gentle embrace. He works with the Base, the Sacral and the Navel chakras which are associated with our basic needs, our strength and grounding. These chakras also focus on our security, loving relationships, and help to clear lower energies. Imagine a diamond and this shows how Archangel Gabriel shines.

### Archangel Haniel

'Glory of God' Haniel brings feminine moon energies, beauty, harmony and grace into our lives. He helps us to trust our intuition and develop our clairvoyance. Like the moon, Archangel Haniel is mysterious and gentle, kind and loving. He soothes emotions and I feel he sings as he does this. He opens us up to understand our sensitivity, being empathic yet not oversensitive within our own energy.

### Archangel Jophiel

'Beauty of God'. Archangel Jophiel helps us to think beautiful thoughts helping us to create, manifest and attract more joy and happiness into our lives. He brings us knowledge from the Universe, helping us to learn, grow in spiritual understanding, and helping us to ascend. I feel my Crown chakra tingling when Archangel Jophiel is with me. I can feel the wisdom being downloaded as the thousand-petal lotus of my Crown unfolds. I see a pure golden, yellow light flowing into me, blessing me with wisdom and understanding of the Universe. I believe this Archangel connects to me as a teacher.

### Archangel Christine

Archangel Christine is the divine Feminine of Archangel Jophiel, and together they work with the Crown chakra, assisting us to bring down spiritual awareness, wisdom and understanding. Archangel Christine, like the 'Christ' in her name, radiates gold. She helps those who are on their ascension path and will support our spiritual development with unconditional love. Her energy is soft yet powerful and I love to call her in to help me see everything with enlightened eyes.

### Archangel Mariel

Archangel Mariel oversees the Soul Star chakra and is illuminated in magenta light. This angel helps us to bring forward the wisdom from our past lives and oversees our soul journey. Archangel Mariel, through our past lives, helps us to heal what we no longer need or what no longer serves us from previous lifetimes. I call upon Archangel Mariel to help me guide my clients during their past life regressions.

## Archangel Mary

I love working with Archangel Mary, who is the twin flame of Archangel Raphael, as she brings transcendent love, compassion, comfort and healing. She works with the water and has a beautiful aquamarine light. I call upon her every time I give healing and work with children, including my own. As a mother, teacher and healer, I feel that her amazing calm, understanding and gentle energy is often around me.

## Archangel Metatron

His beautiful golden-orange light helps us on our ascension path, he is the mighty Archangel who oversees our personal ascension and brings spiritual leadership. Archangel Metatron works with children too, which is why I call upon him often so that I can help guide others.

## Archangel Michael

Archangel Michael is the angel of protection, truth, strength and courage. He gives guidance and direction for people and brings in justice. I call upon Archangel Michael in many ways, but mostly to protect me and my energy, keeping me safe and to help clear away any attachments (cords) which no longer serve me and pull my energy down. I visualise his sword cutting the cords and clearing my energy.

## Archangel Raphael

Archangel Raphael is the mighty emerald healer. He helps you heal your physical, emotional, mental and spiritual body. He is also the Archangel to call upon for prosperity and abundance. Working with your Third Eye, Archangel Raphael helps to strengthen your clairvoyance. As a healer, I call upon him all the time to bring and send healing to people, animals and the planet under the Law of Grace.

## Archangel Sandalphon

Sandalphon is the 'Angel of music' and oversees our Earth Star chakra. He works with Mother Earth and helps us to ground. His twin flame is Archangel Metatron and both are the only angels that have ever walked the planet. Archangel Sandalphon helps us to sync with our divine potential.

## Archangel Uriel

Archangel Uriel in his golden yellow light links with the Solar Plexus and therefore he helps us with our intuition, wisdom, self-confidence and self-worth. I can always feel my Solar Plexus spinning when he draws near and I can see his illuminating golden yellow light in my mind's eye. I also feel protected and safe.

### *Meditation to Meet Your Guardian Angel*

*Connect with your breathing. Take a conscious breath, becoming aware of your breathing. Breathe in deeply through your nose and slowly breathe out through your mouth. Breathe in... and out... in... and out...*

*Simply focus on your breath, in... and out... in... and out... Notice your heart rate becoming slower and more relaxed. Breathing in... and out... Calm and relaxed.*

*Take your attention to the soles of your feet. Imagine roots growing out from the soles of your feet and slowly making their way down through the cool Earth. Feel the connection to Mother Earth as they continue to grow deeper and deeper down. Visualise these beautiful roots as they begin to spread wide, anchoring you to Mother Earth.*

*As your roots connect in with the Earth, find some crystals hidden in the soil and wrap your roots around them. The crystals can be all the same or different, it is your choice, but as you are connected to them you begin to draw up their wonderful, healing energy, along with the Earth's grounding energy. Just like sucking through a straw, draw up these energies and as these energies blend with yours through your feet, I want you to send the energy all round your body.*

*As it touches all your muscles, they relax and release any tension held there. Any areas of body which need healing will receive healing as the energy touches it.*

*Now I want you to visualise yourself standing by the river's edge, notice the running water, so clear and watch as the ripples splash over the rocks causing rainbow sparkles. Feel the warm sun's rays gently caressing your skin as it shines down on you. Take note of your surroundings, the velvet green grass, the soft breeze, and the pale blue sky with only a scattering of fluffy clouds. All around you is peaceful and you can hear your heart beating inside your chest. You are calm and relaxed.*

*It is a beautiful sunny day; the flowers of all colours are in full bloom and you can smell their individual scents. If you listen carefully, you can hear the hum of insects.......*

*Notice the small animals, squirrels, birds, rabbits, as they play by the oak tree near you. Watch them a while......*

*A pure white beam appears in front of you. Your energy changes, feel how it gently shifts. Can you feel how your energy has raised and your vibration, higher? Blend with this energy, it is safe.*

*The pure white light encircles you and as it does you notice a figure slowly becoming visible. As you continue to look and your eyes adjust, the figure, which feels warm and kind, becomes clearer and clearer. As the figure stands in front of you, look into their eyes, notice they are familiar. It feels like you have known them all your life; you have, since the beginning of time! This is your Guardian Angel.*

*Ask her to draw closer, as she does, she embraces you with her soft angel wings. Feel the warmth and love which emanate through her.*

*Stay a while together and talk. You can ask her any questions, find out how she has helped you in your life. She will willingly share her wisdom. Her answers may come as thoughts or images, feelings or just a knowing.*

*Your Guardian Angel gives you a symbol, personal to you. Receive it with love and grace. Any time you wish to be near her, think of the symbol.*

*Know that you can come back at any time, she is always around you and close by. Talk with her at any time you need love, guidance or reassurance.*

*As she begins to fade, you become aware of the surroundings around you.*

*Take a big breath in and slowly breathe it out. Breathe in... and out. Wiggle your fingers and toes, and when you are ready, open your eyes.*

## Our Guardian Angels

Archangels oversee our Guardian Angels; they are like the managers.

We all have a Guardian Angel assigned to us at birth, or as I believe, from our first creation. They are constantly with us, ever at our side. They don't judge, they are constantly supporting us as they know our true heart, our essence and our blueprint. They know why we are here, our mission and our karma. They will help to navigate us around the obstacles but won't help us to skip past them unless these obstacles are not assigned to us. Putting it clearer, they our Guardian Angels will steer us in the right direction, but if we are meant to walk through the muddy waters, then they will hold our hands as we enter.

Many people have an absolutely awesome experience when they first meet their Guardian Angel or the angelic realm but I can honestly say that when I did a guided meditation to meet mine, it was wonderful but I wasn't 'blown away' by it. To be honest, I felt like I was reintroduced to an old friend. I have always believed in angels and knew I had a Guardian Angel so it was normal to me. I'd been praying to her all my life. What did astound me was her name, Moonstone. Again it felt completely right, I love moonstone crystals and a few years prior to this experience I asked my mother-in-law to buy me a moonstone pendant. She had asked what I wanted. We were both on a spiritual pathway, and living in Brighton, she has several New Age shops to look in rather than ordering one from the Internet. I wore it unconsciously all the time. The day after my Guardian Angel gave me her name, which came through telepathically, I was standing at the photocopier at work. Another teacher out of the blue commented on what a lovely necklace I was wearing and said, "Is that a moonstone?" I had forgotten I was wearing it, and as I said, I wore it all the time and I saw Imogen every day at school. This was the sign that I had asked for; I had asked for her name to be confirmed and the very next day I received my confirmation.

How we can communicate with the angelic realm?

You may encounter one or all these things at different times or depending on which angel you are connecting with. It is all about practice, and the more you connect the easier you will understand their subtle ways.

- *Changes in our energy* – temperature, goosebumps, shivers, feeling of total calmness or unconditional love flooding through our whole being
- *Visions* – mind's eye or in perfect sight
- *Emotional* – tears, love
- *Numbers*
- *Knowing* – just get a sense that they are with you
- *Ideas* may pop into your mind without thought
- *Hear* them calling your name
- *Sparkles* or flickers of colour or white light

- *Dreams*
- *Syncronicities*

## *Angel Protection*

Archangels are here to help and protect us. I often call upon Archangel Michael with his sword of justice and his enormous energy to keep me protected and to clear away any lower energies that may have attached to me. This quick visualisation is extremely powerful and effective.

> *I call upon Archangel Michael in your beautiful royal blue light and I ask that you clear my aura of any lower energies held there. I also ask that you cut any cords which no longer serve me, for my highest and greatest good.*
> *I call upon you to surround me in a beautiful ball of protection, allowing only love and light to enter and to send back any negative energy as LOVE.*
> *Namaste*

## Invocation and Meditation for the Archangels

Here is a very powerful and beautiful invocation and meditation, which will help you to align with the energy of the Archangels and bring them into your aura. You may care to record this so that you can concentrate on the energy coming into you.

I have chosen one Archangel, but you can call in as many as you like and ask them to bring their gifts to you.

> *I now invoke the mighty Archangel Raphael with his emerald light. I ask that he fills me with healing, prosperity and abundance for my highest and greatest good. I ask that I be given truth and clear vision. And so it is.*

*Feel Archangel Raphael drawing close and feel or sense his energy as it merges with yours. You may receive an image or be impressed with thoughts or words; this is his communication with you.*

*Namaste*

## The Angelic Realm

All angels have a role to play, and although we don't consider there to be a hierarchy, as they are all equally important, there is, however, an order of angels ranging from the most powerful angels to the numerous everyday angels who we communicate and work with. There are nine in total and you have probably heard of some of them.

**Seraphim** – These are the highest order of angels who are the guardians of God. They are sometimes called a 'Choir of Angels' and have six wings.

**Cherubim** – The second highest rank of angels, they also serve God.

**Thrones** – The angels of humility and peace.

**Dominions** – A group of angels who help keep the world in order with justice. They help the other angels to be organised and carry out their work.

**Virtues** – These angels govern nature and are sometimes called the 'Shining ones'.

**Powers** – The 'Warrior' angels help defend against evil (or keep the world at a higher frequency).

**Principalities** – These have command over the lower angels and fulfil God's promises.

**Archangels** – Sent by God to deliver important messages. They can communicate and work with us.

**Angels** – They deliver our prayers to God and to us here on Earth. They are the closest in vibration to us so they can communicate and interact with us more easily (when asked).

## Part Two

# Understanding Spirituality

In the coming chapters I would like to explain my understanding of several key aspects which will underpin your spiritual development and give you practical advice to deepen your connection to the spirit world, your loved ones, guides (including animal guides) and the angelic realms. This is by no means an extensive list, however, studying these aspects and weaving them into my practice has proved essential for me and I continue today with these exercises.

## Chapter 6

# Understanding Spiritualism

Spirituality means something different to everyone; to some it is about religion but for others it is non-religious based. My understanding of spirituality, and yours may be different, is that it's about connecting to something bigger than ourselves. It is more than the meaning of life which sounds 'cheesy' to me, but simply how we connect to the Divine (Our Creator, God, Source), nature and the Universe. For me it is about understanding the world around us, being in tune with the Universe and ourselves. It is the understanding that we are all one yet, also, uniquely different. Our soul is our connection to the Divine, we are a spark, a fragment of a larger soul energy. It is our connection to Source, so looking inwards and aligning ourselves with our true essence will help us to evolve and grow spiritually.

Raising our vibration means replacing old patterns or lower thoughts we have about ourselves or others which are no longer serving us with better ones. When we raise our vibrations, we are attuning ourselves to the Universe, to Source or the Divine (whichever you wish to name it), so we can follow our natural state. It is about returning to who we are, our authentic self. Spiritualism for me is about being connected.

When I first opened up to Spiritualism I was and still am a Christian, however, although I love churches and cathedrals, I prefer to sit quietly inside them absorbing the wonderful energy and peace they exude whilst marvelling at their truly magnificent structures, than listen to the teaching of the Bible. I have felt this from an early age and now I understand why.

Some spiritualists believe in a set of rules and lead their lives according to them, even teach them, just like the Principles of

Reiki. Although I believe and share the importance of these rules, I feel uncomfortable about the title 'Rules' as it makes me feel like it is a religion. I have included them here anyway; as I said, I do follow them, but don't consider them a list to check in with, but more of how to be a spiritual person, a better person, a person who is compassionate, understanding and decent.

## Journey to Spirituality

1. **Pure Potential** – We are all consciousness. Connecting with our highest consciousness (Higher Self) is the purest wisdom and one of our greatest gifts. The importance of this is to find the answers within, and as our Higher Self, our Monad or our true essence holds our blueprint for who we are, we can't go wrong if we listen to it. Beneath the soles of our feet is our Earth Star chakra which holds our true potential; connecting with this energy will keep us aligned to our soul and our highest potential. Connecting to Earth and the Divine enables us to be perfectly balanced, and by trusting our intuition, following our heart, we can be true to ourselves and carry out the role we came here on Earth to complete.

2. **Generosity** – Life flows, energy flows, it is the flow and exchange of energy which keeps us moving, evolving and growing. Generosity isn't about money, it is the time and energy, the love and kindness we share with others. What we give to others will return to us 3-fold. What we give out, we receive, and if we can do this gracefully, then the energy of life will flow generously.

3. **The Laws of Karma** – What we sow, we reap. What goes around, comes around. You would have heard these sayings many times, but they are true. When we send out love, peace, happiness, it is boomeranged back to us. Be mindful to give

out what you wish to receive, send out kindness instead of negative energy. Karma: several Eastern religions understand karma as a cause and effect, either positively or negatively, and that we can carry this 'energy' over into other lifetimes or incarnations. My understanding of karma is this, if we can live by these Spiritual Laws, we can live in harmony. However, life is a journey and we need to experience situations to grow and evolve spiritually. It is therefore important that we must experience the good and not so good – the difficult, the painful, the upsetting. How are we to know and be grateful for the light, if we haven't experienced the dark? The Yin and Yang of life. I don't believe that if we are 'bad' then we will be 'punished' in another life. I see it as an accountability, that we review our actions and learn how we have made others suffer – consciously or unconsciously. Then we make amends, right the wrongs. This can be in this incarnation or another.

4. **Least Effort** – Every action generates a flow of energy which returns to you. I noticed this as a mother and teacher, if I was calm, then my children or the children in my class would be calm. If I jumped up and down in frustration or was stressed, the environment changed and became louder or argumentative. It was a comment we were wisely advised in university, "A noisy teacher, a noisy classroom." This was definitely true, I worked with both.

5. **Intention and Desire** – What we wish for is nestled into our consciousness; if we dream of it, we can attract it if it is for our highest and greatest good for ourselves and others. Another phrase I have heard of many times which I truly believe is, "Something meant for you will never pass you by." This reminds me of fate and how the Divine orchestrates your life. Free Will is a gift to humans, however, if it is meant to be, it will come to you in the end, no matter how long or how often

you push it away. Fate has a funny way of constantly placing the opportunities beneath your nose. Keeping our intentions positive and attainable will also ensure the Universe hears you loud and clear. Remember too that those intentions are for our spiritual growth, they must never interfere with other people or cause havoc with other lives. Always state intentions for the highest and greatest good for all.

6. **Detachment** – Being openminded, surrendering to fate and allowing life to unfold with trust that it will be for the best. Detachment is not being aloof! More detaching from drama and learning to trust the Universe knows exactly what you need. From my experience, all the worry in the world will not make something happen faster, nor will it change the outcome. It will be what it is meant to be, so have faith.

7. **Connecting with Your Dharma** – We are all unique and we must express ourselves in our own unique way with our gifts and talents that we were given. (Dharma: in Buddhism it means 'cosmic law and order'; in Hinduism it means the right behaviour and social order.) We are all unique, perfectly so, even our quirky or annoying traits harmonise with our brilliance and create a balance. Celebrate your gifts, use them to guide you through this lifetime and support others. We are who we are, and if you don't like who you are, then you alone can change that. If you are a negative thinker, you can alter your thought patterns. If you don't like your shape, colour or something you can't change, then change the way you see yourself and learn to love the positives.

So, you see the 7 Laws of Spirituality are not a list of dos and don'ts but a guide on how you should live your life. I feel that if you are a decent human being, being empathetic, loving, giving, understanding and true to yourself, then you will be leading a spiritual life. It should be a natural way of being, not forced. It is our essence, and if we are true to ourselves as God intended, then we are on the right path. Stay true to yourself and learn to love YOURSELF and OTHERS who are sent to walk this journey with you.

## Chapter 7

# Understanding Spiritual Language

In this section I will guide you through some ways which will help you understand spirituality and how intuition works.

To develop your psychic intuition and deepen your gifts you need to constantly be raising your vibration to a higher level, heightening all your senses as it is an integral part of our psychic development. In doing so, we can focus on the '5 Clairs'. These include:

- Clairvoyance
- Clairsentience
- Clairaudience
- Claircognizance
- Clairgustance & Clairalience

Connecting to your soul will help you to raise above the mundane aspects of life and steer you through lower emotions which ultimately hold you back from fulfilling your true purpose. Using your 'clairs' will provide you the tools to do just this.

Let's look at these clairs in more detail below.

**Clairvoyance** is when you see things in your mind's eye like a vision, daydream, movie playing in your mind or dream when you sleep. It is clear seeing except you can see it with your physical eyes. Imagine your forehead is a screen, when you receive images psychically or from Spirit you will see them projected there. You may even see a little movie sequence being played out on your inner screen as you begin to see events which have happened. However, not everyone will see this; it is more common to simply see the individual images. Every time I use my clairvoyance, I ask Spirit to help me sense or know a little more about the images I'm being shown. It is like a constant communication between myself and a friend. Remember to listen too, often images are accompanied by a sense, a thought, a feeling or a timescale such as an important date. For example, when I am shown roses, I ask Spirit whether it is because the person in spirit or my client favoured roses above other flowers or whether it symbolises a birthday, anniversary or a passing or indeed a special memory. Both my father and mother-in-law have a strong connection with a rose bush, my mother-in-law's ashes being buried under one in my front garden.

Combining clairvoyance and spirit communication in this way is key for evidential mediumship and flow, otherwise it becomes a string of objects where the sitter must fill in the gaps. It is the medium's job to understand, interpret and make sense of the information they are receiving. It will take time to develop your spiritual senses so don't be hard on yourself, be guided instead.

**Exercise to strengthen your clairvoyance:**

- First you need to clear and cleanse the mind and your aura.
- Focus on your breath, breathing in through your Third Eye and out of your throat. Breathing in through the heart and back out through your throat – repeat as often as necessary.
- See a golden, shining light flowing through each of your chakras from your Crown chakra to your Earth Star beneath your feet. See yourself in a column of golden light.
- Take your attention to your forehead and see it as a screen; any worries, doubts, negative thoughts written on the screen can be wiped away with a cloth until it is clear.

- Now visualise your Third Eye as a diamond with many facets. Clean and polish your diamond until all the smudges have been removed and it's shimmering and reflecting rainbows as the light catches it.
- As the image of your diamond fades, focus once more on your screen. See an image begin to materialise, concentrate on it until it gets clearer and more defined.
- Maybe you can see a colour – understand if this brings an emotional or physical meaning with it.
- Interpret the symbolism behind the image for yourself – what is its message for you?
- Let the image fade, thank the understanding it has brought you.

*This exercise can be practised on other people to strengthen your clairvoyance.

**Clairsentience** uses your physical, mental and emotional body. You know when you are linking in through clairsentience when you get a feeling, a sensation or sense a change in an area of your body e.g., you may feel your throat suddenly get tighter or you may cough and instantly you know that something is different with your throat. You know this is linked to someone else as your throat was fine seconds ago. Healers are naturally clairsentient, they can 'feel' areas within other people's bodies or detect emotional aspects which need healing. When communicating with Spirit, they will often impress their character or an aspect of their personality on to the medium. I have experienced this myself and seen this happen to many other mediums. When a medium suddenly uses phrases that they don't usually use, stands in a certain way or becomes agitated, then you know they are receiving evidence through clairsentience. I have read for many clients who had strict loved ones or were formal in their earthly life and they have made me sit up straight, they made me hurry up and communicate quicker, and they have messed around with my evidence because they have had a sense of humour. I love being clairsentient as it makes my medium real. I am able to connect better with both sides of life and bring through amazing evidence. I feel clairsentience is a powerful way to help show emotions and I often get a whoosh of love for my sitter from their loved one; it's like a virtual hug from the other side. I have witnessed first-hand the power of these emotions when a simple word, character trait or aspect of their character shines through. It gives not only validation but reassurance that they are safe in the Spirit World, proof for them that their loved one has continued life on the other side and is still watching over them and guiding them. Laughter is a huge healer and a phrase or saying passed from spirit to loved one can lift their mood. I have laughed my way through readings before and have been thanked for enabling their 'mum, dad, friend' to be literally in the room with us sharing the energy and space! That's why I love my gift.

**Psychometry** is the art of reading the vibration or the energy of an object which has belonged to someone else. I was told during my training that you should only link into this energy psychically; however, I see nothing wrong with holding a person's grandma's ring and telling them what I am receiving. It is my opinion that this experience can bring a loving connection to the sitter, bridging the gap between the living and the departed. If connecting to a deceased loved one brings love and reassurance, how can that be wrong?

**Exercise to strengthen your clairsentience:**

- First you need to clear and cleanse the mind and your aura.
- Focus on your breath, breathing in through your Third Eye and out of your throat. Breathing in through the

heart and back out through your throat – repeat as often as necessary.

- See a golden, shining light flowing through each of your chakras from your Crown chakra to your Earth Star beneath your feet. See yourself in a column of golden light.
- Ask your Guide to draw close to you.
- Ask them to move around your energy – feel where they are standing each time.
- Sense how wide your energy is, you can use your hand to feel this too.
- Ask a loved one to blend with your energy now. Ask them to show you how they passed or an ailment they experienced. Feel it within your own body as they impress it upon you.
- Repeat as often as you wish – you can even ask other loved ones to blend with you to deepen this experience.

*Make a note of the ailments and how they made you feel, this will become your 'Clairsentience Dictionary' for future reference.

**Clairaudience** is when you hear things in your mind like when you can hear yourself thinking, hear a song that is on a loop in your mind, or like when you hear in your dreams. When we communicate with spirit or our guides, remember they don't have a voice box, so it is more natural to sense their thoughts, to hear your mind saying the words. In readings, I can often hear the spirit world calling out mum, dad, uncle etc. It is also possible to hear names. Sometimes names can be tricky to hear, and you will just get the first initial or first blend sound. This can be because the name is foreign for you; you haven't heard it therefore it is not in your vocabulary. Parents will often say 'mum' or 'dad' as this is how you know them; you would rarely call your mum Christine or your dad Martyn. Another example was when I was giving a reading to a lady and I could hear her dad's 'belly' laugh, it was deep with a strong African accent. I knew this piece of information, I didn't hear it in my own ears, but I sensed it and felt it within me. The evidence was immediately taken with reassurance I had connected with her father.

People with a strong life bond will often be telepathic. Your close connection will enable you to read their thoughts. How many times have you gone to ring a friend and they text you or call before you dial their number? That is an example of telepathy. Reading people's emotions is another way to communicate through telepathy.

Telepathy is the art of communicating with the mind, connecting with the subconsciousness. We are all vibrational beings, and just like a radio, we can tune into similar frequencies.

**Tips to strengthen your clairaudience:**

1. Listen to others carefully.
2. Let others speak without interrupting.
3. Listen to the sounds of nature.
4. Don't question your thoughts.
5. Sense where the voice is coming from.
6. When listening to music, try to identify the individual instruments.
7. Spend time in silence, tune in to the silence.
8. Be calm – empty the mind and stop the barrage of thoughts.

**Exercise to strengthen your clairaudience:**

- First you need to clear and cleanse the mind and your aura.
- Focus on your breath, breathing in through your Third Eye and out of your throat. Breathing in through the

heart and back out through your throat – repeat as often as necessary.

- See a golden, shining light flowing through each of your chakras from your Crown chakra to your Earth Star beneath your feet. See yourself in a column of golden light.
- Listen to the sounds around you – tune in and focus on the sounds.
- Hear your favourite music in your mind.
- Listen to individual instruments as they play in the song.
- Think about a loved one (here or in spirit) – hear their voice, their laughter, their favourite saying.
- Hear these sounds – drums, the washing machine on full cycle, a bell, birds singing.

**Claircognizance** is a 'knowing'. It is as if a piece of information has simply been picked out of nowhere and been dropped into your mind. You don't know how you know, you just do. This 'clair' is the one which requires the most trust as many intuitive people feel like it's their own mind, their own thoughts and they have made it up. I say once again, trust. I find this way of working is amazing; it is quick, specific and accurate as your mind hasn't time to intervene or change the words. Often, I will be talking about something relevant which is happening around them or about somebody close, when my words will just pop out from nowhere. It makes me laugh when I gasp and say, "Sorry, but can you understand that piece of evidence?" And I love it when they most certainly do.

The quicker you give the images, say the words, describe the sensations, the quicker spirit will follow it up with another piece of information. This is the trust which is given by spirit to you as a gift. If you have strong claircognizance, then you will be creative, have inspired thoughts or can answer questions you haven't heard of before. I used to do this as a child watching game shows or quizzes – I wasn't as clever as others thought, I simply was tapping into my Higher Self or my guides for the answers.

**To strengthen your claircognizance, all you need is TRUST, but also:**

- **Sit with a notepad and pen, quieten your mind and allow yourself to drift, shifting your consciousness.**
- **Write anything which comes to mind but don't analyse it.**
- **Continue until the flow stops.**
- **Practise often, it will become easier.**

*Automatic Writing is how people use and tap into claircognizance.

**Clairalience** is the sense of smelling, like smelling smoke when nobody is smoking nearby. I've experienced this sensation many times. You may be able to smell your loved ones, everyone has their 'special' scent, or you may be able to smell things which spark a memory. Often mediums can smell or taste food that a spirit wishes to give as evidence too. I once tasted apple pie which was totally relevant to my client. I have tasted humbugs, mints, sweets, chocolate. This 'clair' is called **Clairgustance**, and both are amazing pieces of evidence and so exciting when received.

**Exercise to strengthen your clairalience/clairgustance:**

- First you need to clear and cleanse the mind and your aura.
- Focus on your breath, breathing in through your Third Eye and out of your throat. Breathing in through the

heart and back out through your throat – repeat as often as necessary.

- See a golden, shining light flowing through each of your chakras from your Crown chakra to your Earth Star beneath your feet. See yourself in a column of golden light.
- Call upon your loved one, and as they blend with you, smell their familiar scent, it may be anything from smoke, perfume, soap to powder puff.
- Ask them to give you a taste of their favourite food (cake, pudding, chocolate/sweet or drink).

I am often asked, "How do I connect to Spirit?" "How is it that I change when I start giving messages from spirit?" (My eyes go funny a friend once reported.) Well, it is all about how we shift our consciousness. I usually focus on my breathing, taking in deep breaths, clearing my mind and calming my body as spirit can't connect to a busy mind or stressed medium. When I feel still, I focus on opening my chakras, then call upon my guides and loved ones to come close into my energy (auric field). I sit awhile with them blending with their energy with the intention of raising my vibration. If my energy is low, then guides, angels and spirit can't blend with me as they can only lower their vibration to a certain level. Once this is established, I then mentally invite them to work with me. Shifting consciousness is a process where I move myself from my conscious brain into my subconscious, like walking through a doorway. Although working in my subconscious, I am still aware of my bodily functions. Think of it this way, have you ever driven to a place you drive to regularly, and upon arriving, you are amazed you are there because you haven't remembered any part of the journey? That is shifting consciousness, doing things in a haze. It can happen in other situations too, when you are cooking, cleaning, painting, playing music or any activity where you are able to 'tune-out' and complete the task by rote. Therefore, I never remember anything in my readings I haven't been totally aware of in my conscious mind.

When I first started out with my mediumship, I found that my spirit communicators (other people's loved ones) seemed so far away. It was like I was talking to them over the phone in a different room, but gradually, the more I practised I could feel them getting closer. In fact, after a while I began to feel them coming into my energy and I was able to determine not only where they were standing, but that each position had a different meaning. Let me explain further. When I connect with loved ones on the female side, my communicators stand to my left, and if they are from the male side they stand on the right. So, mother's side on the left, father's on the right, and if they are grandparents, the same rule is applied, however, this time I feel them slightly higher, so I know they are a generation above. This can be repeated for great-grandparents too. I feel uncles and aunts above but to the side as if there is a gap between the parent, but again the same side. E.g., my uncle (my dad's brother) would be on my right, slightly apart from my dad but lower than my paternal grandparents. Cousins and friends follow the same energy as the client; however, a cousin stands with the family and the friend is once again further away. The only problem with this that I have encountered is if a friend comes through which was like a sister to them. It's not really a problem, they will usually place themselves as a sister.

Often during my readings, I will get an enthusiastic spirit who is excited that their loved one has come to chat. It would be they who has pushed and pushed for them to come and have made it possible to arrange a date and time with the right medium. They sometimes draw so close that they practically are part of you; this is called blending. When the spirits are so close, when they have merged with your energy the medium can hardly think or feel straight. While this makes great evidence, it slightly takes the medium's control away. At this point, you need to ask the spirit to step back slightly. This is particularly important if these emotions or physical ailments are impressing too strongly on the medium. Unless you desire to work as a channel or through trance, blending is the next best way to establish a deeper connection with your spirit communicator, whilst still maintaining some degree of control.

I have another student who really struggled with this in the beginning. Being strongly clairsentient, she couldn't pass over any other details or messages until they stepped back a little. I showed her that all she needed to do was to acknowledge the spirit's emotions and physical feelings, and then ask them politely to move back slightly so that she could work effectively. Spirit always responds, and once the intense feelings had gone, she could deliver the rest of the evidence and bring through a message successfully.

There are times, however, like I said above, that you can ask spirit to draw closer so that you can feel them easier. In this stage you can ask them to temporarily blend with you so that their eyes become your eyes, their thoughts, your thoughts and their feelings become your feelings. When this blending happens, it is much easier for the communication to take place. Remember though if it is too strong, ask them to step back a little.

Throughout my years of teaching, I often see students stand for ages waiting for a spirit communicator to step forward. You can wait for ages, however, the best advice I can offer in these circumstances is to start talking. Even if the first few things you get can't be understood, the communication needs to be built up, and as soon as you start talking, spirit can blend with you and impress their words and feeling onto you. I remember in my early days when I was afraid to say what I was getting, the link would dry up. If you don't pass on their information, they can't follow it up with other pieces of evidence and you the medium will become stuck. Trust they are there to help guide you through the reading, they want their messages to be passed on, so they are not going to let you down. Use your 'clairs' to guide the reading and say what you get, what you can see and how you feel. One tip, however, is not to become caught up in the story; you will trip up as your ego kicks in. When you begin to get some 'no's', go back to spirit and listen again. Take yourself out of the process. Remember, you are blending with your guides, shifting your consciousness, and not allowing ego to creep in.

One of my students used to get caught in this trap. He was and is a brilliant medium but in the early days he latched on to a memory or situation and began to fill in the holes himself. He got frustrated when he became stuck. By removing himself, finding his confidence within his mediumship, he quickly moved forward. Now his evidence is accurate and his messages clear.

## ABCs of Connecting to Spirit in Mediumship

For the mediums who are new to working with spirit, making connections to the other side can be daunting. Once you are practised and confident with your links, then you can go 'free-style' and find your own way of working, however, if new, then these tips below will help give your spirit links a structure.

- Male or female
- Description of appearance – can include height or body frame, facial features like moles, freckles etc
- Relationship to the recipient (mum, dad, friend)
- Passing condition (what took them over to the spirit world)
- Characteristics/personality
- Names
- Places of importance
- Hobbies or job

- Significant memory link
- Significant dates (birthdays, anniversaries, passing)
- Information about their family
- Message

You are looking to bring through at least 5-6 pieces of information which can be taken before you pass on the message. If a piece of evidence isn't understood, don't panic as this will block further information coming through and lower your energy. If no, ask the spirit communicator to help you understand it in a different way. This is NOT changing the evidence; you must never do that but ask them to give you a little more evidence so it can be understood clearer. Sometimes the receiver needs a little time to remember the information, a jog or more context can help. If you feel strongly that the evidence you have been given is correct, stand firm and ask the receiver to hold on to it as sometimes they will remember later, or another family member will confirm it.

I remember this happening to me once when I was reading for a lady; the specific piece of information could just not be understood. Her nan was showing me something purple which she drew my attention to in the garden. It was very vivid and her nan was adamant I pass this information on to her granddaughter. I asked her to keep hold of it (I never retract my information or change it to fit), and sure enough, later that day I had a text message with a photo to say that she could understand it finally. The picture was of purple flowers she had indeed planted in her garden the day before. She also told me she planted them because purple was her nan's favourite colour!

During a reading, the receiver is so engrossed in the emotion and desperately trying to focus on the medium's words that their mind becomes closed. When their mind relaxes a little, they find that of course the information was right and can't believe how they would have forgotten it.

Pulling it altogether, your connection with Spirit should feel natural, not forced, and it needs to flow. You will in time develop this. It takes a leap of faith and trust in your Spirit helpers but going with the flow enables you to communicate clearly, possibly through the different 'clairs', and your links should be spontaneous. Be guided by spirit. I say this with all honestly as they know what they are doing. Having said that, however, us mediums do have control and should not be overtaken. I find that I blend with the right spirit and their loved ones because it is again about my experiences and vocabulary and I totally trust my guides to bring me those I can help. I can't help if I can't blend and link in with spirit whose life experience is outside my experience. Set your intentions clearly and this will help you in your work.

# Chapter 8

# The Afterlife

My understanding of the afterlife, and yours may be different, is what I have read extensively and learnt through my guides. I have also gleaned understanding through my readings and from the past life regressions I have conducted. I believe when we are about to cross over, our loved ones come to meet us. Our Guardian Angel and guides are already with us, but I believe that our loved ones come to continue the next phase of our life with us. This is so that we feel love instead of fear and to welcome us home. I have heard through my clients that they travel through a bright white tunnel and that when they get to the other side they sit through a 'life review'. This is where they can be shown how their life has panned out, the good they have done but also the decisions they have made that potentially cause upset. I don't believe we are judged but we are held responsible for our own actions. My understanding is that we go through a period of healing and adjustment too.

When we have passed over, the veil between both worlds is thin. This is why when a loved one passes over they can travel back to us easily, and they like to hang around, excuse the phrase, until they believe we are OK. This may even include sending us signs or nudging us to visit a medium so they can confirm they are safe and happy on the other side. As time passes for us (remember there is no time in the spirit world, that we can understand), when not needed as much, they can continue their own spirit learning and development. Even prepare to come back down again, to reincarnate.

I have been asked many times why people pass too soon. Why do they die young or take their own life? Firstly, I'd like to explain that it, in my opinion. it is always the right time to pass. As I have expressed earlier, we make that decision during the planning of our life stage, 'The In-between'. If we plan our lessons, weave our life with focus points and arrange the special people who will either help us to learn the said lesson or support and guide us through it, then we will almost certainly design our own passing in a way that is right for us and those we love.

My uncle died at the young age of 50. He was a twin and he always knew he would die young; his sister didn't share the same foreboding feeling. He also knew he wasn't to see his 50th birthday and share that with her. He managed this and passed to the Spirit World soon after.

Scooting forward many years later, I found myself in the horrible situation of losing my baby. I was in the early stages of pregnancy and had had three previously healthy babies, but this one felt different. I had started to lose blood, but when I went to the hospital, they told me it was OK and that there was still a heartbeat. A week later, I experienced the same thing, and although there was still a faint heartbeat, I knew it was slipping away from me. I remember sending my husband to my parents that night, I wanted to be alone; it felt private between me and my baby. I put the boys to bed, and then around 9pm my TV suddenly switched on but glowed instead of a picture. This grabbed my attention. Then I saw my nan in spirit; she was holding my baby which I knew was a boy and she told me that she had come to get him and would take care of him. In my heart I knew he would come back to me when the time was right. Crying, I remember nodding and feeling thankful that she was there, taking on that role. Then they disappeared. I knew he was going back home. Two years later I fell pregnant again. I had my healthy baby boy back. This was his time to be born, this was the incarnation he was meant to have. He is five years old now.

This experience showed me that not all babies are meant to be born. I believe they come for the experience of connecting with the mother so that they can receive unconditional love. It is also important that the mother blends with her child. In my case, I feel I was being introduced to my child, being told to expect him as I believe he has a special task in this lifetime. I also feel this experience was shown to me so that I could share it.

I have a wonderful friend, Claire, who sadly experienced a stillbirth at nine months. I can't image how heartbreaking that situation must have been, and I honestly believe you can never get over the loss of your child (at any age) but again there is a reason for it to happen. Without sounding harsh or uncaring, it was the bigger soul plan, not just for the baby but for the mother and whole family. The themes of unconditional love, bonding and heartbreak were being experienced by all. The amazing part of this story was that Claire went on to have another two healthy children.

Another delicate area to understand is that of suicide. I am often asked, why do people choose to take their own life? This is such a hard topic to discuss, a delicate subject which brings such pain to the family and loved ones. I have read for several people who have unfortunately experienced suicide and each time I have brought through their loved ones, there is an enormous amount of love. A common message I am asked to pass on is that they are fine and happy and occasionally an apology. Not necessarily because they wished they hadn't done it, but for the pain it has caused. I have been told that it was a cry for help which went wrong, and for some it was that their life was just too hard, and they couldn't deal with it any longer. All the readings and messages are hard to deliver, and I hope I always get the emotion right for the spirit and their loved one. There is the most beautiful honesty which comes through and I feel blessed that I can help bridge the love, and bring understanding, reassurance and healing to my clients.

So why does this happen? It was their time; regardless of the passing situation, they chose to go in that way.

Sometimes suicide can be because the person has incarnated too quickly and wasn't prepared. Maybe they hadn't brought with them the right supportive people to guide them through difficult situations and maybe because they bit off more than they could chew and decided to end their contract, go back to spirit and replan. I also believe that there is much learning for the families who are left behind and not only emotionally, but I've also heard amazing stories of charities which are formed to raise awareness of people with mental health issues and this is a good thing which grows from tragedy. There is a higher purpose and the beautiful soul agreed to be that soul who leaves Earth too soon.

My dad, like his brother I mentioned earlier, also knew he would pass at a relatively young age the same as his father, my beloved grandpa who died at 72 years. He was right, my dad suffered an unexpected heart attack whilst driving home from hospital after a routine check-up. His passing was quick, in a car (he loved cars, especially fixing them) without us being there or hurting anyone else – there were no other cars or pedestrians involved. This I believe was planned beautifully by himself as he was a man who would have hated to have become ill or be a burden. Easily frustrated, he would have loathed losing the ability to move or, dare I say, sit still (he was an incurable fidget!). Dad would have not wanted us to see him injured, nor would he have wanted us to be in a crash with him. It is interesting that my dad, who we were so close to, spent the whole day before with me and my boys travelling to Oxfordshire to look at our new house and investigate several local primary schools. He even persuaded me to go to a local café (not a chain) to have tea and scones for me, and Coke and a chocolate brownie for him and the boys. My sister also had an opportunity to spend longer with him the weekend before when they got lost in Luton, driving around and around – both were his unconscious ways of spending one longer time with us.

So, although a complete shock, he did indeed plan the perfect return back home. I'm one hundred per cent certain he was met by his loving family and the angels too; we never die alone! In the same way we arrive with a Guardian Angel and Guides, we return home with them too.

Children with special needs in my belief are beautiful souls who are highly evolved, here to help us, the family, to understand love, teach us about patience, empathy, strength, courage and resilience. These children can bring families together or can separate them – but that is also the plan as not everyone is ready to devote such loving attention to the child, and maybe the parents were chosen for the perfect genes but not as a contributor in their life.

# Chapter 9

# Light Workers, Star Children and Their Importance

Everyone here on Earth are all light workers, in fact anyone who helps others, the planet and animals, anyone who shines the light and brings healing is a light worker. There are no special powers, just kindness, respect, loving and supportive people who work without needing rewards and do so naturally.

It has been suggested that there are groups of children who have been born during specific times to help humanity. Being incarnated in waves brings support to the planet and its children. The children being born during these times are identified by specific qualities. These children are called Indigo, Crystal and Rainbow children.

Looking at these groups of children separately, Indigo children tend to be spiritual warriors, here to challenge authority, change old ways and break rules which are no longer serving us. They were born between the 1960s-1980s to give the planet a little shake up with their determination and no-nonsense attitudes. They searched for the truth and disliked injustice. Indigo children are often diagnosed with ADD or ADHD. If you look at their auras, they usually hold more purples and deep blues within their energy.

If you have an indigo child or you are one yourself, you will notice that they are quite strong-willed, passionate about things they believe in and will not be deterred. This may come across as 'naughty' or 'challenging', but this isn't always the case. They are free thinkers and will question everything, so are bound to stand out in a classroom and challenge the information they are receiving. Being born leaders themselves, they will have difficulty with authority. Indigo children are truth seekers, they will know if they are being lied to and are usually very open and honest themselves; again this may lead to finding themselves in trouble. They are intelligent, perceptive, empathetic and compassionate (animal lovers) and will no doubt stick up for the underdog. Indigo children are intuitive, creative and want to change the world. They can be loners, or at least, need their own space. Their expectations of themselves and others are high, and they can be idealistic. As I write this and consider myself as a child, I can identify with all the above. I wouldn't necessarily get into trouble and respected my teachers, but that didn't mean I agreed with them and I certainly caused problems at home for needing acceptance, didn't like being told what to do – always needing the last word and challenged the rules if I felt them to be too harsh or unfair!

Crystal children came afterwards to smooth the way with their even tempers, bringing harmony. These spiritual children hold a higher frequency and are very intuitive. These children are sometimes diagnosed with autism and they usually don't speak for the first few years of their life; they are using telepathy to communicate. Crystal children have transparent, clearer auras like crystals.

Rainbow children love to serve others, they are giving and can express their emotions freely. They are gentle yet fearless children, recovering from negativity quickly. Rainbow children are rare and have all the colours' help within their aura.

Star children, as they are sometimes collectively called, are here to help us and our planet through this time of ascension. They originate from different locations in the Universe, and as I said above, have been sent to Earth for a mission, to help us. Star seeds are hugely evolved beings who wish to bring their gifts to humanity.

We asked for their help; therefore it is up to us to protect them. We can do this by helping them become energetically balanced, helping them to remain calm and stay grounded so they can control their own emotions, which they find hard to do. They also bring gifts, usually in a healing form or to teach us to love, stand up for ourselves, justice and honesty. Helping our star children, or indeed you if you feel you are a star seed, to understand their gifts will help make their journey through this lifetime much easier.

Teaching sensitive children about energy, how to tune into their own and how to protect themselves from negative or lower energies emitted from their environment and the people they spend time with is beneficial for them; in fact it crucial. Star children are extremely sensitive and will often have allergies or sensitivities to food and chemicals, so watching their diet and making sure that it is healthy and balanced, organic, if possible, will bring much relief to them. Checking for hidden food and chemicals is also important in helping your child achieve a balanced energetic state.

During my conversations with my guides, I believe that although these star children are currently placed into a category as I outlined above, the guidelines are actually more fluid and interchangeable than that. I have come to understand that it depends on where these star children's origins are from which determines their characteristics. For example my origins are from Lyra and I have trained in many other planet systems, most noticeably the Pleiades. For this reason I am adventurous and like to travel, not fearful of the unknown, drawn to ancient or spiritual places, can be serious, and have a passion for helping others. I also have a strong sense that there is a reason for my existence on this planet. Other Lyran traits which I identify with are that I am drawn to the stars and believe in human potential. I am grateful for my healing qualities which I credit to the Pleiades along with my honesty, my need to 'fix' and 'understand' others, my empathy and my intuitive sensitivity and healing gift.

It is my understanding that regarding these star children, whether called Indigo, Rainbow, Crystal or simply star children from another planet, the support we offer them is the same regardless of names. There are also some similar key identification markers which you notice in yourself or your children.

## Common traits of a star child

- Alertness at birth
- Sensitive to people, situations, places
- Sleeping patterns
- Pick up on energy
- Attracted to the stars, astrology, magical stuff
- Scared of the dark
- Say odd things – get a sense of something or tell you something which hasn't happened or happened before their time
- Emotional – struggles to regulate it
- Big eyes or unusual eyes, deep eyes (soulful)
- Old souls

## Ways to support Star Children

- Connect with the healing energies of crystals
- Use colour healing for emotions and moods
- Learn how to regulate their chakra system
- Essential oils balance their energy, moods and bring about healing
- Meditation
- Earthing – an exercise of placing the soles of the feet on the ground to connect with Mother Earth
- Align their mind and heart
- Use positive affirmations to change negative mindsets

## 14 techniques to Ground and Balance Your Child's Energy:

1) Breathing – calming, deep breathing, brain and organ function
2) Grounding – being outside in nature
3) Yoga – stretches, movement, exercise
4) Sleeping patterns – serotonin, REM sleep, chemicals
5) Affirmations – positive phrases to imbed positive thought patterns
6) Outside – walking, sunshine, barefoot
7) Massage – oxytocin – story massage, taking your finger for a walk
8) Chakra balancing
9) Crystals – holding, sleeping placed in rooms, bathing
10) Meditations – guided and relaxation, calming
11) Identify your worries and triggers, but feed them energy
12) Practise gratitude and being thankful
13) Use positive affirmation
14) Healing

Practising some or all these techniques will help your children to feel empowered about themselves, take control of their emotions, be responsible for their actions and begin to live their lives, true to themselves.

# Chapter 10

# Guides, including Animal Guides, Loved Ones and Ascended Masters

Unlike the angelic realm, guides are people who have lived before and are connected to us specifically for a purpose. We have shared time together with our guides in a past life, or through many, many lifetimes. Each incarnation there would be a different role and relationship; there would also be the role reversal whereby you would be the guide to them too. Each guide has entered into a soul contract with you prior to your return to Earth with detailed plans as to how they will support, teach and lead you during your time down here. Remembering that during each incarnation you are earthbound, your mission is to learn, grow spiritually and address your karma. Earth is the quickest way to evolve; it is the hardest classroom where we can learn many lessons, so most of us choose to do our learning here, despite claiming that we are never going to return, as it can be for some too painful and difficult. Have you ever wondered why some people have such terribly hard lives whilst others float through theirs? My understanding, put briefly, is because people who have seemly easy lives are either new souls (this is evident as they have no real understanding of spiritual things), or they are old souls having addressed most of their karma and are here to help others manage theirs. These are the people who seem to understand everything and are wise – not intelligent but have a wealth of knowledge and usually spiritual (but not always). The people in the middle are in progress and often, as I said earlier, the more difficult the life, the quicker they can ascend. It perhaps pays to cram your lessons into less lifetimes. Once we have returned home, however, we return back to our larger soul for healing, and from this, we understand why our life was as it was, we understand the choices we made and how much we have evolved. Our outlook changes. It is the human mind who wishes never to come back, not the soul!

Our guides know exactly how to help us and were chosen for their attributes, their qualities. Now as guides have 'walked the earth plane' they are not perfect. We don't all have famous or highly intelligent scientists and philosophers, and we certainly don't all have the classic Native American, Ancient Egyptian Pharaoh or a High Priest or Goddess. Our guides are down-to-earth souls with normal names, but they are highly trained and would not be assigned to us unless they could help us in all areas. They are masters at keeping us on track, guiding and steering and listening to us. They are the ones who pop ideas into our heads and help us channel inspirational work, depending on our Soul Plan. We are here on Earth to grow, however, we are also here to teach others and assist others on their life missions and work through their karma.

How many guides do we have? That is not an easy question to answer. Some believe we only have one or two, others believe that we have different guides for different reasons. Seeing as though I have seven, I believe we have several or as many as we need. My understanding is that we have a main guide that has been assigned to us at birth, and that when we need them another guide will be welcomed. Roberto my Franciscan monk and the first one I met has been with me since birth and Daybreak my Native American guide has been with me for many years. I have the two healing guides who I named Bill and Ben; they are a sensei and a Tibetan monk, but because they come together, I am unsure who is who and it doesn't matter. Guides don't care about labels and names, they are just pleased to be recognised, asked to help and to be listened to. I know this as they still come and help me with my healing work. In fact, when they are around, I feel two cold hands on my back. They also appear in my readings or when chatting to people; it's their sign to me that that person needs physical or emotional healing. My other guides have different roles, but I don't really understand specifically how they guide, however, I'm grateful they do, and I feel proud to have them around me.

Guides are not just people; they are animals too. I have a wolf, a magnificent black jaguar whose soft glossy coat I can feel just by closing my eyes and asking her to draw close, and an osprey. I thought he was an eagle but he's not (he gave me three signs), and he helps me with my clairvoyance. I have had many confirmations to prove their existence. I am the most sceptical medium, believe me, and they have shown me sign after sign after sign to prove themselves. Guides come at the right time for our understanding and some will only stay for as long as we need them. I believe my monk, Native American and my wolf are here to stay throughout this lifetime, but the others may move on. I hope not but they may.

Under the title of 'guides' there are our wonderful loved ones. Our grandparents, parents, family members and friends who we can all call upon to help us. I believe that my Grandpa Jack is one of my main guides who used to sit in the corner of a room during my spiritual development to make sure that I was being told the correct information. In fact, every time I do spiritual work or teach, he is with me and no doubt helping me write this book. He was a Virgo like me and very precise, so I totally understand his wish for me to 'get it right' too. I wasn't his favourite grandchild, but I remember vividly how he felt, smelt and the warmth of love that he gave. I'm honoured he has taken on this guiding role, and although he was heavily into the church rather than spiritual, his heart was pure, and he was intelligent. I trust him completely. My dad has also engineered my spiritual development since he passed in 2016 and he joins me when I'm teaching in my development circle. Again, I'm blessed with having my beautiful family with me, helping me from the 'other side'.

Our spiritual team therefore is made up of Guardian Angels, Archangels, Spirit Guides, Animal Spirit Guides and our loved ones. Some people are also guided by elementals – Earth spirits. All of them combined make up our special network and have the exact gifts, knowledge and understanding necessary and the love and know-how to look after us and guide us through the ups and downs of life, however, always for our highest and greatest good, because after all, we are bound by our own soul mission. Within our soul mission, we have chosen to have these challenges in our life and have orchestrated together with our guides, loved ones, friends and colleagues how these challenges will play out, including the difficult people we meet and will learn from. It's an amazing reminder that we are not alone, we are never alone. How lucky are we? We just need to listen and watch out for the subtle signs they send us. Humans were granted 'free will' so although we have all these wonderful guides, we can choose not to listen to them. Some of us do, but I feel by not listening, we just extend our earthly existence by having to come back again and get it right or 'learn' the lesson. My mother-in-law, a truly inspiring and spiritual lady, often commented, "Why did I choose this life for me? I'm not coming back again." However, I know that now she is over there in the spirit world, she will totally understand why she did in fact choose her life and probably congratulated herself with just how many lessons she learnt. She has probably ticked off a chunk of her karma and will be ready to come back after a little healing. This is because we can see the bigger picture. For now, though, she is looking after her family, keeping them safe and sending them love.

Apart from the above, Ascended Masters are available and ready for us to call upon them, in fact, they are waiting for our call. Ascended Masters, like guides, have lived on Earth and have incarnated many, many times. They are important, highly developed spiritual beings who have undergone a series of spiritual transformations called initiations. We can ask these magnificent beings for help and guidance just like the angels; they are here for everyone.

I am introducing my favourite Ascended Masters below, the ones I work with regularly and the ones I feel drawn to and feel a connection with. There are an abundance of Ascended Masters and everyone will be drawn to different ones depending on your life mission or religion/upbringing.

**Mother Mary** – is the Divine Mother of Healing and with her calming blue, pink or magenta ray, she brings love, comfort and compassion. I call upon Mother Mary every time I give or send healing. I love to ask her to come close and work with the children I see within my Calmer Kids role, and I often ask her to look after my four boys. Like Archangel Mary, she is warm and comforting, and although I sense her gentle energy, I know she is powerful. In previous lives, Mother Mary was also Isis during Egyptian times.

**Jesus** – with his amazing golden-white Christ Light, is Lord of Karma. Every time I see or say 33, he draws close. He is a wonderful healer so again I call him in whenever I am giving a healing treatment or working with children.

**Quan Yin** – carries the pink ray of transcendent love. She is the Goddess of Mercy and brings love and compassion whilst spreading Divine Feminine Wisdom. As a Rahanni teacher/ practitioner, I call upon Quan Yin and her 51 celestial pink angels when healing. I find her energy most uplifting and powerful, yet calming, gentle and unassuming.

**Merlin** – the mystic magician, alchemist, teacher, wizard in King Arthur's reign. He wears the stereotypical flowing gown with stars, carries a golden staff and works with crystals. Many people believe he has lived as both Saint Germain and Odin to name just two incarnations, and you can probably see why I am drawn to work with him.

**Saint Germain** – carries the Violet Flame of Transmutation and I regularly call upon him to bring his violet flames in and around me, my family, my house, places of difficulties e.g., schools, prisons, hospitals and even countries where there is war. You can also ask Saint Germain and his violet flame to transmute negative situations and people. His powerful flame turns negativity into positivity and is extremely easy to use.

**Lord Kuthumi** – the World's Teacher. As a school and special needs teacher, spiritual teacher and healing teacher, I call upon Lord Kuthumi to draw close in his crystal yellow ray to help me teach and guide others. He carries the Cosmic Heart and is linked to Venus, so I know that his teaching is pure and from love.

**Mary Magdalene** – the beautiful, but hugely misrepresented soul. She is the Sacred Feminine who works with the heart centre and her essence or gifts to us include intuitive knowing, seeing the truth, standing in our power and to act with kindness and grace. Very important I feel in today's world. She teaches us to look deep within our souls and embrace our shadows. Mary Magdalene invites us to see everything and everyone with an open heart.

**Serapis Bey** – he was a great master in Atlantis and a priest in Ancient Egyptian times. Serapis Bey carries the White Ascension Flame of purity and harmony which helps us to clear lower energies, conflicts and to speak our truth as we travel along our ascension path. When he comes to me, he has the most striking blue eyes, and his energy is loving and gentle. Serapis Bey comes to me when I need to be disciplined in a project or when I need to focus.

As you can see, I have chosen to work with these beautiful, amazing beings to help bring love, healing and teaching to children and people for their highest and greatest good, under the Law of Grace. Their amazing, powerful influence can make such a difference; try it and see!

# Chapter 11

# Your Relationship with Spirit

When I work with spirit, I connect both physically and mediumistically. Being a medium, I link into spirit by shifting my consciousness, to remove my 'ego' and allow spirit to impress visual images, thoughts, feelings, physical sensations into my mind and body. I will also hear them too. Being clairaudient means I can physically hear spirit like the time I was in the kitchen of my old house and I heard clearly, "Be careful, Fergus is at the window." Being in the house alone with just my two boys, I had no idea where this voice came from, however, I listened and responded quickly, entering the living room. Fergus had indeed climbed onto the back of the sofa to look out the window. I don't think he would have fallen, and the window was shut, but I was grateful anyway. Over the years I have often called out to my husband and asked him to repeat what he said to be replied with, "What? I haven't said anything." Although not all clairaudience, however, is as clear and sometimes it is just a word or phrase that you can hear in your head. I am often told "Dad" or "Mum" etc when giving a reading and I say, "I have your dad (mum) here." And when I describe them, they can take the information.

Being psychic, I can pick up on the energy in people's auras and read their past, present and have a sense of what is coming up for them. I understand of course that everyone has free will and does not have to follow any of the intelligence or guidance I, or spirit for that matter, am giving them, as they can use their 'free will' and choose for themselves which route to follow. I am both 'told' information and can sense their emotions. I know when something is not right with a person and I don't just mean physically; emotionally too because I'm a healer and am clairsentient, being able to pick up on other people's energy.

Many of you will be able to do this too. Remember the time you entered a room and felt the atmosphere? Or the time that your friend told you she is fine but you could feel her pain. This is how we use our senses; it is just a healer or clairvoyant or medium will have fine-tuned this ability and it's heightened.

## Steps to develop your relationship with Spirit

1. Practise holding your hands in front of you, palms facing, about half a metre apart. Slowly move your hands together until you can sense a pushing or tingling sensation. You are feeling your own energy.
2. Ask a friend to stand with their back towards you. Holding your palms out, move slowly towards them until you feel a sensation in your palms or they feel a sensation. You are stepping into their energy or aura.
3. Try this again, however, this time, when you enter the auric space, ask them to think of an event, person or situation which causes a strong emotion and see if you can pick up on it. You may have a feeling, see an image, hear a word or just know.

Sensations you may feel – hot, warmth, coolness, tingling, shiver, emotional, goosebumps.

# Chapter 12

# Understanding the Tarot

In my spiritual work, I love to use 'tools' such as the Tarot, runes and colour – reading auras. Ever since my mum gave me those Tarot cards, I have used them practically every day, pulling cards for myself, my family or my friends. I love the way they feel and the energy and accuracy they bring.

The Tarot has always had mixed emotions attached to it. Some love it, some fear it, some think only 'mystics' can read the cards, some think they are the 'root of all evil' and that they're linked to the devil. You need to make your own mind up about it, and hopefully, by the end of today you will see that anyone can read the Tarot and use it successfully for yourself and for others. This brings me to mention that some people believe you can't read the Tarot for yourself; I disagree. I understand that you can interpret the cards to suit yourself or to rationalize the outcome in a slightly more positive way, however, I have been reading the Tarot for myself for about 15 years and I have been amazed at how I've managed to choose, at random, topical cards every time! Both relevant and insightful.

The Tarot is a message or a map of how we can achieve greater fulfilment in our lives, through a balance of emotional and material aspects. When we have a problem, we often can't see the options available to us and which choices to make. The Tarot can help us and guide us through them. In the pictures we have a set of windows through which we may look at life which depict many legends and stories from mythologies, astrological and archetypal significance and esoteric secrets from a wide range of backgrounds. As you become familiar with the Tarot, you will be drawn deeper into the imagery, and it will speak to you. Hence, the 'intuitive' Tarot.

Mastering the Tarot is not about learning all the meanings, but by delving into the imagery, feeling the cards and listening to what they are saying. This comes with practice and patience.

The Tarot can be traced back to 1440 in Italy, and it was believed that it was originally created as a game for the Nobles. It was only centuries later that it was used as a divination tool.

The cards were originally called the Trumps and in the second half of the 15th century the cards became standardized. Many people wanted to eliminate the Death, the Tower and the Devil cards as they offended many, in particular, religious leaders, who tried to ban them.

Early packs were painted and there were only a few of them. Nowadays, they have been used as inspiration to create other oracle cards such as angels, fairies, power animals. These cards do not follow the traditional structure as they lack the suits and numbered cards, but they have replaced some of the more negative imagery.

In my view, oracle cards with only positive images can create a false understanding of a situation, and that in all events, honesty is the key and advice/warnings are needed if the querent wants to be developed and be guided.

In the 1800s, a French priest, Eliphas Levi (1810-1875), inspired an occult revival as he thought the Tarot was the key to the Bible, the Jewish Kabbalah and other spiritual writing. He attempted to link the 22 cards of the Major Arcana to the letters of the Hebrew alphabet.

AE Waite (1857-1942), an English Christian occult philosopher, broke the Order of the Golden Dawn and founded his own school of Mystical Thought. Working with Pamela Colman Smith, he created a deck of Tarot featuring images and scenery on all 78 cards. These were the first pack I ever worked with, and I still have them today, although I don't often use them.

One of the most important things when deciding to learn the Tarot is the selection of your Tarot pack. Take time in this selection and look at the images first. You may be drawn to a pack, be recommended a pack or be given a pack, but ultimately you need to feel comfortable with them. How many Tarot packs should you have? That's up to you; as you become more familiar with oracle cards you will explore the various versions and may want different types for different situations. I have loads, but only use three in my work with clients. I have Archangel cards, Ascended Masters cards, animal cards, dragon cards and crystal cards, which I use for myself and occasionally for others. All my cards I was drawn to; they are beautiful sets of colour and imagery.

The Tarot is made up of 78 cards. Twenty-two cards form the Major Arcana and 56 cards form the Minor Arcana, or the suits as they are often referred to. The Minor Arcana (suits) are made up of four suits, Wands, Cups, Swords and Coins. These in turn are also linked to the elements.

Wands – Fire          Swords – Air
Cups – Water          Coins – Earth

## The Major Arcana

There are 22 cards in the Major Arcana which tell a story of his journey through his life. Observing how he feels, the challenges he faces or the people he meets on his way will be key in how you will interpret situations for the querent. They are also linked to the planets; see the table below.

0 – The Fool – Uranus
1 – The Magician – Mercury
2 – The High Priestess – Moon
3 – The Empress – Venus
4 – The Emperor – Aries

5 – Hierophant – Taurus
6 – The Lovers – Gemini
7 – The Chariot – Cancer
8 – Strength – Leo
9 – The Hermit – Virgo
10 – The Wheel – Jupiter
11 – Justice – Libra
12 – The Hanging Man – Neptune
13 – Death – Scorpio
14 – Temperance – Sagittarius
15 – The Devil – Capricorn
16 – The Towers – Mars
17 – The Star – Aquarius
18 – The Moon – Pisces
19 – The Sun – Sun
20 – Judgement – Pluto
21 – The World – Saturn

## The Minor Arcana

There are 56 cards in the Minor Arcana which are divided into four suits as mentioned previously. The cards show different everyday situations or personality types at work in our lives. They indicate aspects connected with having, thinking, being and doing.

**Wands** – Fire – Growth (energy, action, power)
**Swords** – Air – Action/State of mind
**Cups** – Water – Emotion (feelings, reactions, desires, memories and hopes)
**Coins** (Pentacles) – Earth – Money (work, security)

## Layouts and Spreads

There are many, many ways of laying the cards out to read. Ultimately, you will find your own method which works for you. I came upon mine simply because I couldn't remember the positions of other people's.

Spreads usually follow a pattern, **Past, Present, Future:**

When cards appear in the spread upside down, you can do one of two things. Turn it around (which I do) or read it as a more negative/exaggerated meaning. I believe there are enough cards in the deck which cover all situations and emotions, you don't need to read positive cards as negative. What do you think?

## How to give a reading

- Create a quiet, welcoming environment (music, incense, crystals, lighting)
- Manner – be honest, sympathetic but detached
- Remember to explain how you are reading for them and they shouldn't feed you
- Supply tissues and water
- Other suggestions

Remember that when making a prediction it is a snapshot of what you feel at that moment in time and that the querent has their own free will and oversees their own life.

I suggest that to strengthen your connection to your cards, you hold them regularly, look and use them frequently until they become your friends. I trust my Tarot cards, and to me I can always rely on them, just like good friends. Looking after your friends is also important, so make sure you look after them with respect and store them safely. I keep mine in a velvet drawstring bag, but you could also store them in a wooden box, wrap in them in coloured silk cloth or place a crystal on top of them to charge them. Before I use my cards, I give them a quick shuffle then a gentle knock to clear any previous energy. I also occasionally run them through some cleansing incense.

There is a saying or belief that it is bad luck to let other people touch your cards. I'll let you decide how you feel about that, but how will you be able to read them if they haven't put their energies on them! The only time my clients can't touch my cards is when I am giving phone readings or Zoom readings.

# Chapter 13

# Understanding Crystals

Since I was a teenager, I started to collect crystals. I used to put my collection in my room and would often look and hold them. I knew they had meanings and energy attached to them, that was my intuitive understanding, but what, I had no idea. They eventually gathered dust, and by the time I was in my late teens, I had forgotten about them and they disappeared. I don't know where they went. My understanding now though is that their energy was always a part of me, I was meant to use them and when the right time came, I would bring through this subconscious knowledge, passed down from previous incarnations and now I still have them everywhere, but the difference is that they play an enormous part of my life, particularly in self-development and healing.

## Introducing Crystals

All minerals which have grown within the Earth hold powerful energies which have been stored for millions of years being shaped by volcanic heat and waters seeping into the ground.

Crystals have been used by man for protection, healing, rituals, meditation, cosmetically, medicinal and other practical purposes since the beginning of time. Archaeologists have found crystals in prehistoric graves in Europe, the Middle East, Russia and Africa. The crystals were probably amulets and talismans, used for protection and spiritual/religious rites. Among the crystals found were amber, jet, turquoise, carnelian, quartz and garnet. The Ancient Egyptians used crystals mainly for health and protection. They were found in the tombs, as amulets, in headdresses and made into jewellery. The Egyptians also ground crystals to use them as make-up. Lapis lazuli was considered a royal stone. It was often ground down and rubbed onto the crown to help get rid of spiritual impurities. Malachite was used to help the pharaohs rule wisely. It was also used to help eyesight and to have inner visions. Green stones generally signified the heart of the deceased and were used in burial rituals.

Native Americans used crystals for healing, ceremonial and spiritual purposes. Some Mexican indigenous tribes believed the souls of people who have led a good life will enter the crystals. In China and Japan, quartz was thought to represent the heart or essence of the dragon. Dragons were thought to have great power, be wise and highly evolved. Jade is also well known to be used in China and Japan; it is considered to assist friendship and draw love.

In India stones were regarded as having great spiritual and emotional powers. Moonstone for example was a sacred stone and believed to arouse love, whereas the ruby was considered to hold value and was known as 'King of precious stone'.

Crystals are known in all religions and were mentioned in the Bible. The most notable being in Exodus, where the High Priest Aaron (brother of Moses) was instructed by God to make a breastplate from crystals to be worn for protection and wisdom. Crystals are mentioned in the Bible approximately 200 times.

Note, that some crystals are man-made, combined or are altered by heat, but even though they have been manipulated, they still carry an energy, a vibration which is healing.

## How Do Crystals Work?

Whilst holding a crystal in your hand, you may be able to feel it vibrate ever so gently as they hold subtle energy within them. To some it may feel like a tingling, to others a scratching sensation, burning feeling on the palms or simply holding a crystal may just make you feel more positive. This is because crystals have a physical, balancing effect as they realign atoms in our body.

The energy our Earth puts into the creation of crystals transforms into power for healing properties. Holding one of these gifts of nature, allowing it to resonate with our own energies, allows it to assist us in our healing. This shows us just what powers crystals and gemstones have. The energy and nature of gemstones is universal energy. When our energy systems breakdown, e.g., under stress, crystal energy can help to rebalance us.

## Types of Crystals

Crystals are classified as minerals but not all minerals are crystals. Crystals have an atomic structure which is regular and forms a crystalline pattern. Minerals are inorganic in nature, although amber, coral and pearl (which are organic) are included.

Crystals are members of the quartz family and are described as living computers: they absorb, store and send out energy. The quartz group of minerals goes to make up 12% of the Earth's crust. We can divide the quartz family into several main groups.

- Clear quartz crystal (rock or mountain – highest expression of the mineral world and symbolises perfection)
- Rose quartz
- Amethyst
- Citrine
- Black tourmaline quartz (clear quartz with inclusions of black tourmaline)
- Rutilated quartz (clear, smoky grey, brown with needle-like inclusions of rutile)

These quartz crystals usually have a six-sided form ending in a termination point. On rare occasions, you can find clear quartz with two termination points, one on each end. This is called a double terminator point and these crystals have very strong healing powers as they can draw and release energy at both ends. Therefore, a terminator is used by healers so they can direct the healing energy into their client through the healing session. The more pointed the apex, the more perfect its healing power. Energy is drawn into the body of the crystal and passes through it and out of its termination points. In order to release the crystal's energy, it needs to be stimulated by body heat, direct sunlight, contact from other crystals or have been programmed.

## Chalcedony or Microcrystalline Quartz

These can be dull and glassy in appearance. They are generally found near the surface of the Earth where the temperature and pressure are relatively lower.

- Aventurine – quartz coloured with iridescent green mica
- Chalcedony – white, blue, grey
- Chrysoprase – opaque apple green
- Bloodstone – opaque dark green with spots of red jasper
- Carnelian – translucent red, orange, yellow
- Moss agate – translucent milky white with moss-like inclusions
- Tiger's eye – gold-yellow to gold brown

## Agates

Most agates occur as nodules in volcanic rocks or ancient lava. If cut transversely, they show a succession of parallel lines, giving them a banded appearance.

In many traditions, agate is believed to cure the stings of scorpions and the bites of snakes, soothe the mind, still thunder and lightning, and bring victory over enemies.

- Blue lace agate
- Fire agate

- Moss agate
- Carnelian agate

## Inclusions Found in Quartz Crystals

Many quartz crystals vary in colour and clarity. This is because of very small amounts of dispersed impurities (inclusions) found within them. Clear quartz becomes a deep violet colour (amethyst) due to inclusions of iron; if titanium or magnesium is found then you get rose quartz; or there can be needle-like inclusions of rutile forming a hexagonal pattern, then you get star rubies. Holes, bubbles and irregularities are often found. Rainbow quartz contain air and water, producing the effects, and radioactivity found at great underground depths absorbs the ultraviolet light changing it into smoky quartz.

The colour of stones can also be changed by heat; this can make their appearance lighter over a period (so remember not to leave your amethyst in the sunlight).

**In general**
**Agates** – grounding, stabilizing, strengthening
**Jaspers** – nurturing
**Quartz** – healing, balance
**Chalcedony** – peace making

So you can see just how amazing these little gems of the Earth are and how they support our minds, bodies, emotions and spirits to grow, heal and expand our consciousness. I wouldn't be without my crystals, and they are usually my first place to go when advising others how to move through a difficulty.

# Chapter 14

# What Are the Chakras?

The word chakra comes from an ancient Sanskrit word meaning 'wheel' so many see each chakra as a spinning wheel which controls the energy coming into your body and being released from your body. They are energy portals which are made up of nerves and are linked to the major organs. The chakras can have a huge impact on our emotional, physical, mental and spiritual well-being, and are aften discussed as being 'too open' or 'closed'.

The understanding of our chakras can be traced back to 1500 BC and are often the topic of conversations in New Age and yoga philosophies.

There are many chakras all over our body, however, many people often only concentrate on the main seven in terms of healing and spiritual awareness. There are twelve chakras which are important in spirituality and connecting to the Divine, but that is for another time, another book! Let's get the understanding of the major seven before advancing.

Although we are looking at each chakra at one time, know that all chakras are important and that they all relate to each other, so if you work only on one or two specific chakras, then you will create an imbalance.

Lower chakras are connected to earthly things and upper chakras are related to spiritual things; however, all the chakras are relevant and necessary to the mind, body and spirit. They work together and need to be aligned.

Because our energy centres are so sensitive, they can regularly get blocked, so some ways to clear our chakras are sea salt baths or to splash salt water over the chakra, walk in water or barefoot on the grass, shield and clear ourselves daily with white light.

## Base Chakra/Root Chakra

The Base chakra is connected to your overall feeling of balance, sense of safety, security, confidence and abundance. Being grounded means that you have a sense of being in your own body, not feeling spaced out. Being grounded has an impact on your health, life purpose, career and relationships. When your Base chakra is unbalanced then you will experience a sense of not knowing what is going on around you and the sense of feeling vulnerable, not connecting or finding it hard to listen to others as so much is going on in your head. When your Base chakra is balanced, you will be more focused, and you are taking control of your own life.

Colour – Red/ruby

Emotional – Anxious, fearful, insecure, feeling unsafe, stressed, lack of confidence.

Physical – Linked to the adrenal glands: glands produce adrenaline when stressed to face danger and give you strength, fight/flight response. Over time this has a knock-on effect to other organs.

- Back/spine problems
- Kidneys
- Adrenal fatigue – low sugar balance, tiredness

Crystals – Garnet, red jasper, haematite etc

## Sacral Chakra

The Sacral chakra is located between your spine and your navel. It is linked to the adrenal glands which are home to the testes and ovaries. It links in with your addictions and impulses.

Colour – Orange

Emotional/Physical – Fertility problems and sexual issues are two physical areas where an imbalanced Sacral chakra can manifest itself.

Crystals – Carnelian or any orange stones

## Solar Plexus Chakra

The Solar Plexus chakra is linked to the digestive system/gastric/liver/gall bladder and is about our own personal power. It is your psychic centre too – 'gut' feelings and where you hold your worries and fears.

Colour – Yellow

Emotional/Physical – Stomach and gastric issues, liver problems and gall bladder issues. The pancreas and adrenal glands secrete adrenaline under stress.

We will feel more confident and feel good about ourselves if the Solar Plexus is balanced. Remember, women can be powerful and feminine as well as men.

Crystals – Tiger's eye, citrine, yellow jasper, smoky quartz

## Heart Chakra

We feel with our heart and should trust what it is telling us. If you look at the word heart, you will see 'ear' in the middle. This is because the heart hears the truth, and if we are wise, we will listen. We need to learn to trust our heart and follow it, even if it is scary. If you do, then life will flow; if we don't then we come up against obstacles. We can only flow and hear if we keep it open.

The heart is all about love, agape love, which is the essence of knowing that we're one. Life has ups and downs, sometimes we can close the Heart chakra as a result of pain and hurt. It is an instinct to shut down the light within it. We are here on Earth to love and remember that true love can never be abusive.

Colour – Emerald, green/pink

Emotional/Physical – Issues surrounding love, matters of the heart, emotions and the immune system. It is also linked to the lungs and arms.

The Heart chakra is linked to your cardiovascular system, energy and the endocrine glands, the thymus.

Everyone has been hurt, it is how you deal with it that matters; you can become angry, bitter, judgemental, isolate, sour or not trust others. Or you can learn from the experiences and let the heart teach us our life lessons. This will make us stronger so that we can survive and trust again.

Crystals – Malachite, fluorite, green crystals

## Throat Chakra

It is all about communication and getting in touch with your truth, to commit to what you are saying and finding your voice. If you are having trouble writing your book, composing a song or writing a letter, then it could be that your Throat chakra is blocked. When open, it helps singers to sing and speakers to communicate.

Being linked to the thyroid gland, it helps to regulate our energy. It is wonderful that the thyroid gland is shaped as a butterfly: it has two wings and a butterfly is a metaphor for spreading your wings and flying. Releasing your fears about becoming a conformist and speaking your truth in a way that is kind, noting the feelings of others.

Colour – Sea blue, turquoise

Emotional/Physical – Hoarseness or sore throats are a sign of a blocked Throat chakra as are issues related to the thyroid gland.

Crystals – Aqua aura, turquoise, blue lace agate, lapis lazuli, any blue crystals

## Third Eye Chakra

The Third Eye is the window of clairvoyance. The Third Eye is seeing with your mind's eye. When someone describes something, you get an image in your mind, you can visualise it or see it in your dreams; this is how clairvoyance shows us.

Colour – Rainbow of colours and moon essence, indigo blue

Emotional/Physical – Physical sense of sight.

Crystals – Lapis lazuli, clear crystal quartz (reflects the vibration of all the colours of the rainbow)

## Crown Chakra

The Crown chakra is found at the top of your head and extends upwards. Its Sanskrit name means 'a thousand petals' and is our connection to the Divine, to Source.

The Crown chakra is the pathway of the psychic sense known as claircognizance or 'clear-knowing'. It downloads information; you may sometimes just know things even though you don't know the person or have just met them. It's like you have just been told information. For example, you can fix something intuitively.

Healers are claircognizant (as well as using other 'clairs'). When they meet with their clients they can link in with them and know what is wrong with them immediately. People who are claircognizant also get a million ideas in their mind. Some run with the ideas, others talk themselves out of it; it depends ultimately how much you trust the information you are receiving.

Colour – White/opalescent

Emotional/Physical – The head, brain.

Crystals – Apophyllite, clear quartz, amethyst, sugilite

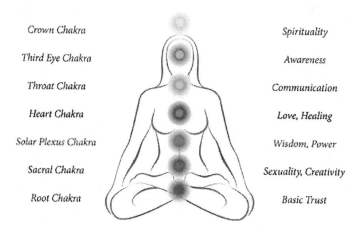

| | |
|---|---|
| *Crown Chakra* | *Spirituality* |
| *Third Eye Chakra* | *Awareness* |
| *Throat Chakra* | *Communication* |
| *Heart Chakra* | *Love, Healing* |
| *Solar Plexus Chakra* | *Wisdom, Power* |
| *Sacral Chakra* | *Sexuality, Creativity* |
| *Root Chakra* | *Basic Trust* |

## Practical 1 – Balancing each chakra with a crystal

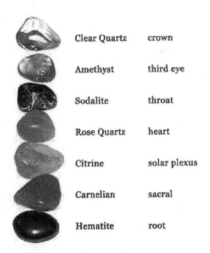

| | | |
|---|---|---|
| | Clear Quartz | crown |
| | Amethyst | third eye |
| | Sodalite | throat |
| | Rose Quartz | heart |
| | Citrine | solar plexus |
| | Carnelian | sacral |
| | Hematite | root |

*It is important to know that crystals respond to thoughts, not verbal instructions, so allow your thoughts to be clear and positive. Believing and trusting the crystals to help will heighten their energy.

## Practical 2

Place the crystal in your hand with the point facing your body. Calm your mind and breathe slowly for a few minutes. Draw in white light through your Crown and concentrate your thoughts on instilling the crystal with healing and balancing power. Imagine the white light being drawn down through you and into your hand, filling the crystal with the white light energy.

Hold the crystal over each chakra one at a time, breathing in the crystal's energy.

## Crystals: Colours and Their Energies

| Colour | Energy | Help | Stones |
|---|---|---|---|
| Red | Warming, energising, stimulating, grounding, brings strength, courage and perseverance | Anaemia, depression, infertility, aches and pains | Ruby, Garnet, Bloodstone, Tiger's Eye, Red Jasper |

| | | | |
|---|---|---|---|
| **Orange** | Stimulates the digestive system, aids low immune system, exhaustion, helps moodiness, brings joy and happiness | Kidneys, lungs, menstrual cramps, infertility, arthritis, blood | Carnelian, Coral, Amber |
| **Yellow** | Nervous system, aids digestion, helps with decision making | Motor difficulties, lymphatic system, mental stimulant | Yellow Topaz, Citrine, Yellow Jasper |
| **Green** | Love, fidelity, beauty, environment, wealth, luck | Shock, heart, lungs, respiratory system, high blood pressure, allergies | Emerald, Jade, Malachite, Green Aventurine, Moss Agate, Green Jasper |
| **Blue** | Idealism, justice, career, promotion, long-distance travel, house moves, marriage, prosperity, peace | Thyroid gland, throat, fevers, inflammation, cuts, bruises, scalds and burns, eyesight, communication disorders | Aquamarine, Blue Topaz, Sodalite, Lapis Lazuli, Turquoise |
| **Purple** | Spiritual, imagination, dreams, psychic powers, intuition, teaching, counselling, healing, psychic protection | Headaches, ears, hair, sinusitis, easing childbirth, addictions, phobias, allergies, insomnia | Amethyst, Opal, Moonstone |
| **Pink** | Reconciliation, mending quarrels, happy family, kindness, girls entering puberty, new love | Glands, ears, stress, PMS, ulcers, insomnia, babies, children | Rose Quartz, Rhodonite, Morganite |
| **Black** | Transformation, peaceful endings, grief, sorrow, destructive influences, blocking negative or harmful forces, psychic protection | Pain relief, constipation, IBS, shields from side effects of invasive treatments (X-rays or chemo) | Black Tourmaline, Onyx, Jet |

## Choosing Crystals

All crystals have a life-force energy and an elemental consciousness that lies dormant until it is awakened. It can only be awakened by linking into the Deva of the stone through its highest self; it's true love that will awaken the energy in the stone.

A stone will stay with you if its energy is needed, after which time it will remove itself. Sometimes you will be unable to find the stone and it will reappear later. This is because you are now in tune to its energy and are receptive to its healing power.

One of the best ways of acquiring a stone is by being given one as a gift. You should do this too: if you no longer need its energy, give it to someone. When buying a crystal, be careful; at fairs or in shops, many people have touched them and by doing this have placed their own energy on the stone creating conflicting vibrations. You must also remember that unpolished stones are purer in spirit and won't have been touched as often; it is often the least attractive stone that has the strongest healing power.

When you do choose a stone, use your intuition and see which one you are drawn to. You could place the stone in your hand and feel the vibrations (tingling, hot, cold). You will instinctively know!

## Cleansing Crystals

Once you have acquired a crystal, you need to cleanse it to get rid of any negative energy. There are several ways to do this.

- Bury it in the ground overnight.
- Wash it in the sea or in a glass of pure water to which a tablespoon of salt has been added.
- Wash under a running tap.
- With incense.
- With your mind – place the crystal in your left hand with the point facing away from you. Breathe in and still your mind. Ask for the stone to be purified and cleansed and

that all negative energy be expelled from it. Visualise all the negativity being sucked out of it and away (white light).

Once you have cleansed your crystal, you will need to keep it near to you for it to blend with your own vibrations. You could keep it in your pocket or sleep with it under your pillow.

Caring for your crystals is important too. Hold them regularly, keep them in natural light (not in a drawer), and they should be placed in direct sunlight/moonlight for a few hours every week. Do not place them on a magnetic surface as their properties could be altered. If other people touch your crystals, or you have been working with them, make sure you cleanse them again. Crystals which are full of energy or need recharging will feel different.

## Healing with Crystals

When healing with crystals, your collection should be quite large, and you may require several of the same stone. You can buy chakra stones which are useful to have.

The first stone you purchase should be quite large as this will become your generator crystal. This crystal will activate the smaller ones when not in use. Place the smaller crystals in a circle around the generator crystal in a circular pattern.

It is also a good idea to have a quartz crystal relating to each of the four elements – Earth, Wind, Fire, Water.

- Clear quartz crystal
- Rose quartz
- Citrine quartz
- Smoky quartz

## Crystal Elixirs and Gem Water

Gem or crystal water (elixirs) work in the same way as homeopathic and flower remedies; it uses the subtle vibrations of the stones to help balance one's life. It is empowered water which has been charged with the spiritual energy of the crystals. Drinking crystal water/gem water daily will help to build up your immune system and will help in your body's defence against colds and flu.

**Elixirs/Crystal water:** Place a small quartz crystal which has already been cleansed into a covered container of water for a few hours or overnight. Ask for the elixir to be "created for the greatest good and purest purpose to bring the healing/help/protection in the best way for..."

The elixir will keep their full power for 24 hours in the fridge.

PLEASE MAKE SURE THAT YOU CHECK THAT YOUR CRYSTAL IS SAFE TO MAKE ELIXIRS WITH.

**Gem water:** This is the same but this time using a cleansed gem.

## Programming a Crystal

Healing crystals can be programmed to act as amplifiers, to absorb and reflect energy. You can programme crystals for gifts, distance healing and you can programme a crystal to 'self-cleanse' itself.

### Practical

1. You can hold the crystal in your left hand with the point facing upwards. Now hold your right hand over the top of the crystal and concentrate on the white light entering your Crown chakra and flowing down through your left hand, up through the base of the crystal and out of the top. Your right hand acts as a circuit. Now ask for the crystal to be programmed for one of the following.
   - Balance and harmony
   - Harmony and healing
   - Protection
   - Health and happiness

- Changing negative energy
- Releasing blockages in the chakras

Accompany the programming with imagining yourself/ person being treated in perfect health.

2. When programming a crystal for a gift, create a strong mental picture of the person who is receiving the crystal. Programme the crystal for specific healing or a colour which will aid the healing (see below):

- Red – energy, vitality, strength, grounding
- Orange – bring joy, release emotional blocks
- Yellow – bring expansion, wisdom, clarity of thought, soothe the nerves
- Green – create harmony and balance, open the heart, love
- Blue – peace and serenity, trust and loyalty, intuition
- Indigo – inspiration, purification, meditation
- Violet – aid meditation, spiritual growth, creativity

3. Distance Healing – place a photo under the crystal and ask for/visualise the person receiving healing for their highest good.

4. When using your crystals in healing they would have absorbed vibrations from the emotional, mental or physical body of the patient. To prevent these energies contaminating other crystals, you or other patients, you can programme your crystals to self-cleanse themselves to stop you having to keep doing it. Follow steps from number two and ask the crystal to cleanse and purify negative energy. Visualise this too.

You will know if a crystal needs cleansing as you will feel a burning sensation in the palm of your hand when holding it or have negative images when meditating with it.

## Practical

*Healing an issue with a crystal (choose a crystal and hold it in your left, receptive hand).*

*Siting quietly, focus on your breath. As you take deep breaths in and out, feel your mind clearing, your body centring and your heat slowing. Relax your muscles, allow yourself to sink into the chair you are sitting in and calm your energy and emotions.*

*Bring your crystal to your Third Eye. As you breathe in, breathe in the crystal's soothing energy. Focus on a situation, past or present, that you wish to heal.*

*See everyone involved and feel their emotions. Sense how it makes you feel. See how it affects your current life and relationships. Sit with this emotion for a while and when you are ready, in your mind, express to that person or to the Universe how YOU feel. Say any words that you wish to say, pour your heart out and release any pent-up emotions. Release feelings, pain, guilt, words – let it all out.*

*Now take your crystal to your heart and breathe in once again its gentle, healing energy.*

*Visualise the situation or the person in a positive light. See them understanding your emotion or see the situation clearing. Then with forgiveness, see them turning around and walking away from you in a bubble of golden white, pink light.*

*Take a big deep breath in again, and as you exhale, slowly familiarise yourself and your surroundings, and when you are ready, open your eyes.*

## Dowsing

Dowsing is the art of divination which can be used as a tool for predicting outcomes. Traditionally, people used to use pendulums (or rods) to dowse for water underground such as springs and wells, but today it is largely used in fortune-telling.

The pendulum is a weighted object, either metal or crystal, attached to a string or chain. When held above the body it connects with the mind, the subconscious mind. This means that we are not thinking about the outcome of our question, we are allowing our Higher Self to provide the answers. Thinking, connecting to the conscious mind will have a different result as we can make the crystal swing through will alone. Therefore, I rarely use pendulum dowsing for myself. I tend to only use it for others and in healing to detect whether chakras are open or closed or if there is an imbalance within a person's energy field.

Firstly you need to connect with your crystal, establish a code for Yes and No; this could mean the pendulum swings clockwise or anticlockwise, or like me circles for a yes and swings side-to-side for a no. A maybe for me is when the pendulum does nothing as it is unsure. Once you have established your code (and it will be different for others but always the same for you), then ask permission to dowse. That's only polite and it tells us if it is for the highest good.

Dowsing is a lot of fun and you can ask it many things, but remember it is a tool. Get to know your crystal and build up a respect with it.

### Things that you can dowse for using crystals
- Finding lost items
- Yes/No questions
- Maps – direction
- Healing
- Spiritual

### Don'ts
- Become reliant
- Dowse for others unless you have their permission
- If you are unbalanced emotionally or physically

BE open-minded.

Always use the pendulum for the highest and greatest good of all.

## Crystal Healing Treatment

Crystal healing treatments realign the body's energy fields, opening the chakras to promote an overall feeling of well-being. Crystals are placed around the body or on specific areas which work with your electromagnetic force fields. The most common crystal healing is balancing the chakras.

All treatments should begin with opening and balancing the chakras.

### Starting:

- Place should be warm, quiet, soft music playing.
- Client should remove any jewellery or metal objects and wear loose clothes.
- Work in the North/South direction (this aligns the body to the Earth's magnetic field, enhancing the flow of energy). Head – North; Feet – South.
- Tune into the client's Higher Self, hold your hands over their head and ask them to be healed for their highest good.
- Give thanks at the end of the treatment.

### When giving a treatment you will do one or more of the following:

1. Clearing – negative/blocked energy.
2. Instilling and Balancing – replacing the negative energy with positive vibrations.
3. Expanding – awareness/spiritual development.

### Clearing

You will need six crystal points and a generator.

- **Seal of Solomon** for several minutes

- **Clearing and Strengthening technique**
  - Choose a stone for each **chakra.**
  - Use a **large clear quartz** crystal (facing towards the body – balances; facing away from the body – clearing).
  - With the clear **quartz crystal facing down,** place a **rose quartz between the legs pointing up.**
  - Using a **small clear quartz in the right hand,** make small harmonious **circles down the left-hand side** of the client's body and **up the right-hand side. Connect** the crystal to the **top** and **bottom** crystal. **Repeat 3 times.**
  - **Leave** the client for **10-15 minutes, then** make notes.

## Practical – Opening and Balancing Chakras

### The 7 Major Chakras

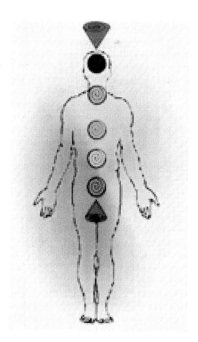

Crown Chakra
The Third Eye Chakra
Throat Chakra
Heart Chakra
Solar Plexus Chakra
Sacral Chakra
Root Chakra

### You need 7 crystals:

- Place **7 crystals** over the chakras – they don't have to be the same colour as the chakra, but they often are (see diagram).

- **Link** the outside crystals with a crystal wand to form a **protective seal (or double terminator).**
- Run **the wand** up from **feet to head**, over the chakras – do this **5 times.**
- **Balance each chakra** with your hands/pendulum:
- Crown and Throat
- Third Eye and Heart
- Throat and Solar Plexus
- Heart and Sacral
- Solar Plexus and Base
- To **instil energy,** use the crystal facing down and **rotate** in circles over each **chakra.**
- To **clear** the **chakras,** hold a **clear quartz crystal in your sending hand and rotate.**
- **In addition, you can scan** the person's etheric (aura) field and feel for any imbalance and hold a clear quartz crystal over it for as long as you feel intuitively is needed.
- **Leave the client** for around 10 minutes before bringing back their attention.

## Selenite

Crystallised Gypsum is colourless and looks like it is made up of needles. It is very brittle, so don't leave it near small children or animals. It is a very powerful crystal which absorbs negative energy from people and around the house.

You can use selenite to:

- cleanse the aura – selenite brush (practical)
- align the spinal canal
- regenerate cells by pointing it at the affected area
- assisting healing of epilepsy (can hold it in their hand during a seizure if possible)
- balancing chakras – Base to Crown, front and back (practical)

## Crystal Pendulums

Using your pendulum (establish 'yes' and 'no') can help detect imbalances in the body. Move the pendulum over the body (chakra as well as limbs, feet, hands), and if the pendulum moves, either place your hand over it or keep the pendulum there until it stops. When you have finished, check the body again by moving the pendulum over it.

If the pendulum keeps moving in the same area, then place a crystal on the spot and check later.

## Treating Animals and Plants

Animals – All animals with four legs have three main chakra points or energy centres: at the top of their head, halfway along the spine and at the base of the tail. You can use a crystal pendulum to balance the energy. Animals will move away when they have absorbed enough of the healing energy. Alternatively, you can place a crystal in the animal's basket or attach it to its collar. For fish, place a crystal in the aquarium or add the colour to the environment to energise the water. As always, choose the crystals/colours intuitively, however, please remember that some crystals are poisonous and you will need to check this before adding them to water.

Plants – Quartz crystal is an overall enhancer and works by placing it on top or in the soil.

## Crystal Grids

Crystals carry universal energy and help the flow of your life, each different yet all powerful and important. Crystals naturally balance, store, transmit, focus, amplify and transmute energy.

When placed together in a pattern, called a grid, the energy is amplified. The arrangement of any number of crystals in a geometric pattern, designed with a specific focus or intent, is important. Crystals are vibrating constantly, and they react and communicate with each other and listen. They work to create the specific energy required.

Crystal grids help us to attract healing, positive energy and situations into our lives. Other benefits are cleansing, protection, releasing blocks, bringing love and friendships, abundance, work, security, spiritual awareness, goals and dreams AND lots more.

### *How to Start*

First set your intentions, be specific about what you want to achieve or attract. Once you have done this, choose a pattern from below. You can draw it on paper, in chalk on the ground, painted on wood etc. These patterns mimic patterns found in nature and are the most powerful for channelling.

**Seed of Life** – associated with growth, harmony, sincerity and truth.

Use for finding a path to goals and desires, good luck, boosting energy and nurturing relationships.

**Flower of Life** – associated with self-knowledge, self-esteem and personal growth.

Use for developing self-belief, and to aid studies.

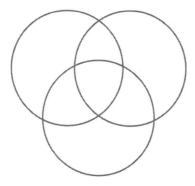

**Tripod of Life** – associated with inspiration and creativity, balance and feminine elements.

Use for making good decisions, dealing with artistic blocks and generating ideas.

**Circle** – associated with protection, safety and belonging.

Use for treating insomnia, promoting teamwork and protecting against psychic attack.

## *Choosing the Crystals*

When selecting your crystals, you can match your intention with the qualities and colours of the crystals, however, it's best to choose your crystals by using your intuition. You may want to choose your crystals according to the colour, their properties or by shape.

**Animals:** spirit animals
**Cube:** solid, security
**Egg:** birth, new beginnings, creation
**Heart:** love, relationships
**Obelisk:** connections between physical and spiritual realms
**Point:** focus, direction
**Pyramid:** energy fields, healing, meditation
**Sphere:** wholeness, completion

## *The Grid*

**Focus Stone** – This is the first one to go on the grid and is usually placed in the centre. It tends to be a bigger crystal than the others.

**Way Stone** – These are the next crystals to be placed on the grid and are positioned around the focus stone. These crystals are used to help you with your obstacles e.g., "What is holding me back?" If it is motivation or energy, then choose red crystals such as carnelian. (See list of crystals in FAQ to help you.)

**Desire Stone** – These crystals are placed at the outer edge of the grid and are the ones most attuned to your goal. E.g., if you are seeking protection, then place haematite there. Desire crystals act as a fence to keep the energy inside. You need a minimum of three.

## *Activating Your Grid*

Before you use your grid, you need to place it in a good location where the elements of water, earth, fire and air can easily flow. Place it near a window so the sun's rays (fire) and the air can get to it. Place a plant (earth) nearby and a bowl of water. To activate it, you will need a crystal wand or a crystal point, clear quartz is good, in your writing hand.

- Focus on your attention as you close your eyes and touch your wand on your Third Eye.
- Point the wand towards the focus stone, imagining it filling with energy.
- Repeat this step for the way stones and the desire stones, and finally for the whole grid.

Each time you pass the grid, stop and focus on its energy, this will increase its power.

## Chapter 15

# Healing Modalities

*Healing is the most special gift we can offer ourselves. Healing the mind, body and soul prepares us to live fully in the present and welcomes abundance of love.*
*– Archangel Raphael*

## Reiki

Reiki is pronounced RAY-KEE. Reiki is a complementary therapy. In the West, Reiki is practised as a form of complementary medicine, where practitioners give Reiki treatments or give themselves 'Self-Healing'. It is largely seen as an Oriental version of spiritual healing, based on the laying of hands and the channelling of a form of energy, or a 'spiritual' energy. This energy can also be used for the benefit of the practitioner.

When Reiki was taught by its founder in the 1920s in Japan, it was taught as a spiritual pathway, a self-healing method and a pathway to enlightenment. Through its journey, Reiki is presented to the world as a treatment technique.

Reiki is not a religion; you do not even have to have any spiritual beliefs in order to benefit from Reiki energy. It is all about moving into a state of balance. This may involve the resolution of some health problems, a change in beliefs or attitudes, it may help to address one's true values and priorities, or finding out what is best for you.

The successful practice of Reiki involves committing some time, regularly, to invest in yourself. The benefits of working with Reiki energy are that it develops over time and builds cumulatively.

All healers use a life-force but not all use Reiki, which works on a specific vibration. Anyone can be attuned to Reiki by a Reiki

Master. It is widely accepted that Reiki not only complements other therapies, but actively increases the strength of those other healing energies.

## What Is Energy?

The energy that Reiki practitioners work with when they treat other people and themselves can be referred to as 'Chi'. An acupuncturist uses needles to encourage the energy to flow through a series of meridians or energy channels that run the length of the body. You may have heard of the Japanese technique called 'Shiatsu'; Indians referred to it as 'prana', and use breathing exercises in yoga to bring the body into balance. However, in India, they are not meridians, but chakras.

The intention with all these energy techniques is that if you can harmonise your energy system, you are putting your body in the best possible position to heal itself on all levels; physical, mental, emotional and spiritual.

It's not just your body that benefits from the flow of energy; feng shui was developed as a way of arranging the living environment so 'chi' can flow freely.

But there is more to Reiki than the energy manipulated by acupuncturists or used in yoga. Reiki is a beautiful energy channelled and it feels loving and nourishing; the more you practise Reiki, the more beautiful it becomes.

Mikao Usui established a simple spiritual system that was rooted in his precepts, his 'rules to live by'. Rather than being an interesting set of instructions to read on a course and to put to one side, Usui's precepts are at the very heart of his system, and it was said that as much spiritual development could come through following the precepts as would come through doing any energy work.

### Mikao Usui's precepts
*Just for today*
*Do not anger*

*Do not worry*
*Be humble*
*Be honest (in your dealings with other people)*
*Be compassionate towards yourself and others*
The Founder, Mikao Usui

Reiki is a huge topic and not one I can or will devote time to in this book. If you are interested in understanding more about Reiki, then I suggest you find a Reiki Master who will introduce this wonderful healing modality to you and start you on your journey.

## Rahanni Celestial Healing

'Rahanni' means 'of one heart', and helps balance the masculine and feminine aspects of every man, woman and child.

I was introduced to this beautiful healing modality by a lady I attended circle with. At that point, I was attuned only to Reiki, but I was keen to learn as much about healing as I possibly could, and because Rahanni was used with the angels, I knew I needed to experience it.

Rahanni is a relatively new healing modality which a lady called Carol Anne Stacey channelled from who she calls the 'higher beings' of light. She was told that this beautiful healing modality was brought to her to give to humanity at this critical time in our existence. It was explained to her that the vibration of Earth had to be raised for this energy to be sustained and because this had now happened, moving from the third to the fourth dimension of reality, we (humanity) were gifted it via Carol Anne.

Carol explains that Rahanni is not based on one religion; it is our natural essence, bringing balance to our mind and body. Rahanni works on a higher level therefore healing in a much deeper way. It vibrates on a pink ray of light, balancing the heart centre bringing forth love and compassion to each individual soul. Although it is thousands of years old it is a 'new' healing for the 'Age of Aquarius'. Bringing truth, love and compassion, helping to change the consciousness and opening the hearts of every man, woman and child. This will help to bring inner peace to the mind and a possible healing to the physical body.

Rahanni is for everyone, but especially children because they are open to these higher energies. It has been known to benefit those children diagnosed with hyperactivity and ADD. Carol explains that the client's body will decide how much of the healing light is required and says many people find their attitudes to life and its difficulties change for the better as a result of receiving Rahanni Celestial Healing.

This beautiful healing radiates on a pink ray and calls in our Rahanni healing guide, Quan Yin and 51 celestial pink angels. I can honestly say that this healing is powerfully gentle, and all my clients have had emotional releases, felt deeply relaxed, serene and come back for more. (If you are interested or wish for a deeper understanding, then please visit Carol Anne Stacey's website, https://www.rahannicelestialhealing.co.uk/.)

If you are drawn to healing but unsure whether to go down a specific route, then please use these exercises below to help you receive and send healing on your own. You are not on your own as you never use your own energy in healing. With any healing, you call upon guides or angels to help bring that energy through you, and using your hands, transfer it to others.

### Guided Meditation for Healing Yourself and Distance Healing
*Sitting comfortably, close your eyes and become aware of your breath. Breathe in deeply through your nose, feel the coolness of the air in your nostrils... and out. Breathe in, filling your lungs, note how they expand out... and out. Breathe in all that is good for you, and as you exhale, release any tensions and worries. Breathing in... and out... in... and out. Your body feeling more and more relaxed. Feel how you are becoming heavier as you let go of all your tension*

*and worries. Let the chair beneath you support you as you become more and more relaxed.*

*Visualise a ball of diamond white light, shining energy above your head, your Crown chakra. Observe it as it expands and gets brighter and brighter.*

*Feel it as it begins to travel down into your body from the top of your head. Slowly bring the white ball of energy down to your face... and neck. Allow it to travel to your shoulders, and as it touches the muscles held there, feel them relaxing and releasing any negative energy into the ball. The white light will transmute the negative energy into positive energy. From the shoulders, send the ball of healing light down your arms to your wrists, to your hands and the tips of your fingers.*

*Feel the healing energy back at your shoulders and send it down your spine, down your chest and stomach to your hips. Feel it continue down your legs from your thighs to your knees... Your calves and shins to your ankles... and into your feet, down to your toes.*

*Your whole body is now filled with divine healing light and energy. Allow that healing energy to completely fill any physical area that needs it.*

*Feel the warmth that it gives as it heals the area it touches, healing it. Allow the healing light to bring peace and healing to any emotional issues or traumas you may have.*

*Stay with this healing energy... Don't worry if the healing light changes colour, it will be the right colour you need.*

*Music/Pause*

*Now visualise yourself holding a ball of energy; as you bring it up to your lips, breathe your healing energy into it. (This is not your energy, but the healing energy you drew down through your Crown chakra.) See yourself passing the ball of healing energy to someone and see them too bringing it down through their Crown chakra until they are surrounded in the healing light. You can repeat this for as many people you like.*

*Watch as they are absorbing and breathing in the healing energy and see them healed, healthy and happy, knowing that the healing has been accepted.*

*Take a deep breath in… and as you exhale, bring your awareness back into the room. Wiggle your fingers and toes, and when you are ready, open your eyes.*

## Healing through Lockdown

During the first few weeks of Lockdown in March 2020, both my husband and I fell victim to COVID. Luckily, although very ill, we did not need to go to hospital. Instead, I turned to my usual intuitive way of self-healing. Each morning I would call upon my healing guides to send me healing for my highest good and I religiously thanked the angelic realms and my guides for their healing I received. To accompany this, I tuned into my body to see which crystals to use. I find intuitively picking crystals is the best way, but if you are new to them, guidebooks are really helpful.

Members of my spiritual circle and healer friends also gave us healing, and we soon improved and gained strength. I was hugely grateful for all their healing too, and as soon as I was strong enough, I began to send out healing to others. I continued this daily for a few weeks, but as the numbers grew, I intuitively understood that more healing was needed so I set up a crystal healing grid and wrote the names of people in need of healing underneath it. I activated the grid and each day added to the energy. I also invited other healers to join me in the distant healing process. Some of them were already doing so, so accepted my invitation and we set up a time to join together in healing thought. Over time, our collective healing became really powerful and we were hearing of more and more people who had made such amazing recovery, even those who were in hospital. It was amazing.

The horrendous symptoms of COVID weren't the only thing people were suffering from. I began hearing stories of people who were affected by mental health issues, and as a group, we sent healing to them too. I recorded a healing visualisation for those who wanted to send healing but were unsure of how to do so, and during the summer our group grew and grew. I am so thankful for this amount of healing being sent out and the lovely healers who joined me.

One day, I had a light-bulb moment or 'download' which I like to call them, and set up a weekly 'Collective Healing' session on Zoom. We meet weekly to receive and send out healing. Each week the theme is different, and we have so far covered COVID, mental health issues, planetary issues, healing for the plant and animal kingdom, rainforests, countries in conflict, specific healing for individuals, angelic healing, and we use sound healing to clear and cleanse chakras and auras and of course incorporate crystals. It is wonderful and still going strong, growing and growing, helping so many people and families.

## Uncle Clive

One morning, just after Christmas 2020, I received the worrying call to send healing to both my aunt and uncle who had been admitted to hospital with COVID. My healer friends rallied too and we sent out lots of healing prayers, sparkles and positive thoughts. But I wanted to do more, so I sat in meditation to enquire what else was needed and how I could support their healing further. Below is an extract of what happened.

*As I settled down into my crossed-legged pose to centre myself with the breath, I set my intention for some healing for everyone who is being affected by COVID. I called upon my healing guides, Archangel Michael for protection, Archangel Raphael and his angels, and Quan Yin and her 51 celestial pink angels. What happened next took me by surprise, for as I concentrated on my breath, I began to watch a scene play out in front of my eyes, within my Third Eye.*

*I could see my uncle and aunt in their hospital beds surrounded in emerald, green bubbles which were slowly rising. This worried me, I must confess, as their souls were moving out of their bodies, but I trusted and continued observing. My breathing was laboured and my body was quietly shaking. As my aunt and uncle rose, they were taken to a healing temple which I instinctively recognised as Atlantis and were lowered into a pool of swirling rainbow colours. My aunt was dipped in and out a couple of times before her soul and the bubble turned a calming and peaceful blue and floated back into her body in the hospital. My uncle carried on rising and falling until he and his bubble turned white and was lifted out of the pool onto a huge bed of amethyst. There were angelic beings all around and priests, but it didn't feel important for me to know who they were. Above the bed, a huge clear quartz beamed white light beginning at his Crown and scanned slowly to his Earth Star at his feet. The purpose of this was to cleanse and clear the body, removing anything bad, for want of a better word. Next, they placed six clear crystal points in a 'Star of David' formation and he stayed there a while whilst also receiving healing from these beautiful angelic beings. I was shown his circulatory system and his blood flowed perfectly around his body. Next a soft, pink, open rose was placed in the centre of his chest, in his Heart chakra.*

*Once this process was complete, he drifted down and back into his body where I could see his face for the first time. He looked peaceful and I became aware that I too was calm and relaxed, not shaking or breathing fast. I knew the healing had worked. From my uncle's bed, Quan Yin stood at his head with her angels surrounding him, filling the room. A beautiful young nurse appeared and was placing her hands over his chest. She was dressed in an old fashioned (WW1 or WW2) white nurse's uniform. I first believed her to be a relative from the Spirit World but now believe she was his guide. She was taking care of him; I knew this was her job and that she was now in charge of his healing. I felt happy and safe to leave him with the angels and Quan Yin, and opened my eyes.*

Around an hour later, I happened to do some yoga and a meditation (weirdly with Quan Yin, Archangel Michael and Archangel Uriel which had popped up on my phone but gave me instant confirmation that the vision I had just had was real). I checked my phone to find out that my mum had texted me and my uncle had moved wards and was to receive a new kind of injection which was in line with the message I received earlier. Although still serious, he was stable. I was and still am totally in awe of the angels, Ascended Masters, guides and loved ones who are able to communicate with us to bring knowledge, understanding and reassurance.

### Distant Healing Bubbles for People and Mother Earth

Sitting comfortably, close your eyes and become aware of your breath. Breathe in deeply through your nose, filling your lungs and then slowly breathe out. Breathe in all that is good for you, and as you exhale, release any tensions and worries. Breathing in… and out… in… and out. Feel your body becoming more and more relaxed.

Visualise a ball of protective light surrounding you. You are safe and protected as you breathe in and out.

Focusing on your breathing, visualise yourself breathing in through your Third Eye and bring the breath around the back of the head as you exhale through your Throat chakra, then breathe into the Heart and bring your breath around your back as you exhale once again through your Throat. Keep repeating this, breathing into your Third Eye, exhaling through your Throat. Breathe in through the Heart and out of the Throat. Keep this figure of eight breathing going, in through the Third Eye, out of your Throat. In through your Heart, out of your Throat.

Call upon your healing guides and the angels – your own, Archangel Raphael, Chamuel, Sandalphon, Gabriel, or any of your other favourite Archangels.

Ask for healing to be activated through and within you so that you can send healing for the highest and greatest good, under Grace. Feel the healing energy building up, and with your palms facing up, feel, see or know the healing bubbles rising and out, floating to the people you know need healing. As the bubble hovers over their Crown chakra, see it burst with amazing, shimmering healing sparkles of golden white and pink.

Send these bubbles to as many people as you know need them; simply say their name or think about them and they will receive them. Send them to the animal kingdom too.

Ask for the healing energy to flow through your entire body, into Mother Earth and see the golden-white shimmering healing light travelling through your roots, connecting to and merging with the ley lines which flow underground around the Earth bringing healing to places which are dense in negative energy.

See your roots merging now with the vast roots of the trees, and as the trees receive this healing, they too receive it for themselves and then send out beautiful healing golden-white bubbles to the planet. See the trees all around the world glowing and shimmering. See the millions of healing bubbles finding people and animals who need them. See the whole world glowing and shimmering with healing.

Sit for as long as you need for the healing to be sent.

Music/Pause

Bringing your attention back to your breathing, taking in deep, slow breaths and exhaling out gently. Breathing in and out, in and out. Wiggle your fingers and toes, and when you are ready open your eyes.

# Chapter 16

# Spiritual Counselling

*Stand in your light with strength and majesty. Allow your thoughts to be of pure nature so you can express who you are to the world. Speak with clarity and integrity. These are your gifts.*
*– Archangel Michael (channelled to me)*

Throughout my journey into spiritualism, I have become aware and now strongly believe that psychic and mediumistic readings, and messages, can bring healing. They provide reassurance, can be guiding and allow insight into your current life and situation. When a client comes to me, they are usually vulnerable. (I do get the group of people who are nosey about their future or want to find out more about their loved ones or development in their own spiritual journey.) I need to therefore understand this and be mindful that their emotions are delicate. My delivery of what I am being told or what I am picking up psychically needs to be given in a way that is both truthful yet sensitive. This is where my counselling skills come in. It isn't counselling like being in a therapy room; it is what's brought forward from Spirit to help provide understanding, give evidence and reassurance. We don't necessarily need to be a qualified counsellor, but we must have an understanding of human psychology and possess a natural level of empathy.

To heal the present, we must first look to our past lives and determine which qualities we have brought with us into our current incarnation. Are these qualities which serve or hinder us? Do we need to keep these aspects of ourselves and refine them, or can we release them and free ourselves from negative recurring patterns which are holding us back?

At this point, we must consider that some of our negative qualities are important life lessons which we must experience, to grow spiritually and emotionally. If we live perfect, happy and harmonious lives, then we do not grow. We would have learnt everything and there would be no need to reincarnate (unless for the sole purpose of helping others).

Looking at the coincidences in our lives – our date of birth, year of birth, our names, maiden and married, the country we are born into, our family and friends – are all ultimately timely for us to carry out our life purpose.

If a character trait is stubbornness, then consider how it can benefit you. Perhaps it may have caused arguments in relationships, but it can be extremely helpful if that stubbornness gives you the fighting passion to beat cancer.

To understand how we can truly know ourselves, we can do several things. We can see our true selves through:

1. Numerology
2. Astrology
3. Past Life Regression
4. Meditation
5. Healing
6. Readings

Below is a testimonial from a wonderful lady who has experienced 'understanding' and 'connection' through healing and reading sessions with me.

*Alison has completely changed my life through her readings, spiritual counselling and teachings.*

*She has healed my 'inner child' by bringing my mother through to explain that she apologized for not giving me enough attention as a child because she was too busy looking after her sick father.*

*(A situation which I was not previously aware of.) Since then, my relationship with my deceased mother has developed through Alison's readings to such an extent that I can now talk directly to her for advice and guidance.*

*Additionally, through her readings, Alison has given my family incredible support, divine guidance and absent healing during challenging times. For example, when my granddaughter was told by the consultant that there was no real treatment for her locked jaw. Alison communicated a message from spirit to ask for angelic healing. Soon afterwards, my granddaughter felt her jaw being manipulated back into place by an angelic presence in her sleep state.*

*Alison has taught me as the matriarch of my family, to ask for divine protection for the family rather than sending them worry. When there was a big fallout between two devoted siblings, during my reading I was given a deep insight into the deeper causes of the rift. I was then able to pass on this information in a sensitive way to help them build a better relationship. Fully understanding that it was not jealousy but a deeply entrenched lack of confidence which was the root cause may have taken years to understand in family therapy. In contrast the reading gave me the simple and loving words to say to the warring duo to heal the wounds of the physical fight and try to prevent the tensions building up again.*

*Several of my friends have started to believe that their loved ones are still around them after Alison's healing and accurate readings. My friend, Jackie, lost her mother aged 8 and was never able to discuss this Polish resistance fighter heroine of a grandmother with her [own] daughter who had always related to her grandmother who was also called Halina. As she passed on Alison's message to her mum about Jackie's mum appearing as a butterfly, Jackie was adamant that butterflies never came near her. Just at that very moment, a butterfly flew into the house landing on Jackie's dress, refusing to budge. This evidence has reassured them both that Halina who died in 1962 as a result of a bullet injury from World War 2 was still around to help them. Another friend who after losing her mother thought she had no family left, only to be told by Alison about surviving relatives wanting to get in touch. Sure enough, she had a phone call soon afterwards from an unknown cousin abroad. During the dark days of lockdowns, Alison's optimism and clear messages from spirit reassured me that positive changes such as the growth of community spirit and people becoming more spiritual brought upliftment. She predicted that after the devastation, there would be "the green shoots and snowdrops and a sense of hope for March 21", which was indeed true. I also witnessed the miraculous recovery of very sick covid sufferers on Alison's absent healing list.*

*My business has been so greatly helped by Alison's teachings and readings because I now understand my soul's mission to work with young people in particular and teach my healing therapies. More young people are now coming to me for treatments and advice. Previously I have always been held back as a therapist because I was too scared to permit my psychic side to come through in my work. These healing readings have helped me on a daily basis by connecting me with my spiritual team of helpers and indeed my Higher Self. When I fell over last week, I was given a stern warning not to multitask on my patio, but I feel that my angels cushioned my fall, causing the minimum harm.*

# Chapter 17

# Numerology

I'm writing this section on 20/02/2020. I thought it would the perfect day to address the wonderful wisdom of numbers.

I have read extensively about numbers, and I have had many, many experiences to prove that numbers, in particular repetitive numbers, hold great insight into what is happening to us at present, the challenges we are facing and the decisions we need to make as well as what is coming up for us, what is round the corner.

Numbers can be found all around us, and I find that for me, they are clues to help my clients in my readings. They help direct me to important dates such as birthdays, anniversaries or the passing of their loved ones. Numbers can help me identify key dates when something may happen, and they can give evidence of ages, numbers of houses, people in their family or children. Sometimes, I am drawn to a specific number because I'm being shown how long they must wait for an outcome to their current situation. Numbers can represent days, months or even years. I simply love the way Spirit uses number signs.

For my own understanding, I also use angelic numbers to help me. I still rely on the above evidence, but with angelic numbers, repetitive number patterns or repeated number sequences, I receive a deeper knowledge of what is happening around me and specifically with me. They become the answers to my inner thoughts, feelings and questions, and they are always spot on. Often, I randomly invite my Guardian Angels and the angelic realm to show me what I need to know; again I get my accurate answer pretty much instantly (or within ten minutes – you have to give them some time to organise it!). Now I am a words kind of person, but I am quickly becoming a fan of numbers through my spiritual development. Like other angelic and spirit signs, numbers are everywhere, and once you tap into their energy, you will be amazed at their accuracy.

Numerology is the study of the relationship between numbers and life. They can be used to understand your personality and can even help you identify your soul path. Specific numbers can indicate your gifts, positive traits and strengths. They can also identify your weaknesses, challenges, obstacles along with any opportunities. Looking deeper into the age-old system of numerology, you can begin to understand yourself and others better. There are four ways to use numerology magic: you can calculate your life path number, your destiny number, your personality number and your soul number. Each method brings different insights.

## Different Methods

Life Path Number – This helps to clarify your strengths and weaknesses alongside any challenges or lessons you may encounter during your lifetime. It is the most common method and one I use myself and with my children, family and friends. I find it hugely accurate and very interesting.

To calculate your life path number, all you have to do is add all the numbers in your date of birth, for example.

*2nd June 1984*
*2+6+1+9+8+4=30*
*3+0=3*
*Life Path Number = 3*

Destiny Number – This method is found by adding up all the letters of your first and surname. (I use both my maiden and married name to find the best fit as I believe, contrary to others, that I was born with a name which was meant for me and I chose to marry into another name. I also believe that by marrying,

I may change as I move into a different phase of my life. Go with your instincts as to which name you'd want to use.)

The destiny number highlights the purpose of your life, what your goals may be and how you can reach them. Again very interesting and helpful.

*SARAH JONES*
*1+1+9+1+8+1+6+5+5+1=38*
*3+8=11*
*Destiny Number = 11*

Personality Number – Add up the consonants of your name to help you to understand your personality, and get a glimpse at how others see you.

Soul Number – Using only the vowels in your name, this helps you to glean insights of your strengths, likes, dislikes and your inner self.

### Number Meanings – my understanding

1 Initial idea or thought. The beginning of something new. Look out for new beginnings. Taking a leap of faith. A new journey.

2 Partnership, a balance of mind and the coming together of a plan.

3 Creativity, as 2 becomes 3. A gathering, social, fun and happiness. I would see this as yellow. (See colour reference.)

4 Indicates the next stage of planning; this is the four walls of a house, a solid foundation. Steady, safe and protective.

5 Obstacles, difficulties, change and growth. The need to shed the old to welcome the new. Changes are on the way, but it will be positive to our soul purpose.

6 Shows family, security and harmony. It shows the triumph over difficulties and balance. 6 is the number of my nan, seeing the number 6 reminds me of her.

7 Manifestation and spiritual – things are taking shape, spirit is around you and working to help you in your goals and dreams.

8 Security and foundations. Aspects within our intellect and our physical life have been completed. It means abundance and prosperity.

9 Spiritual achievement, intuition and humanitarian. Reminds me of my dad, knowing he is with me, guiding me.

10 Wholeness, coming full cycle, completion of a project.

## Characteristics of People

1 – individual, powerful, creative

2 – good-natured, trustworthy, shy, intuitive, patient

3 – attention-seekers, show-offs, charming, entertaining, sensitive, creative

4 – steady, reliable, practical, sensible, solid, honest, dependable, good with money

5 – explores new things, versatile, resourceful, clever, impatient, erratic, untidy, Jack of all trades, argumentative

6 – harmonious, loving, family-minded, peacemaker, gossipy, worrier

7 – spiritual, introspective, mystical, intuitive, knowledgeable

8 – material leader, organiser, successful, self-centred, selfish (Capricorn/Saturn)

9 – humanitarian, intuitive, independent, romantic, passionate, sensitive, high mental/spiritual achievement

10 – completion, end of a cycle – see also 1

## Special numbers – Master numbers which you don't cancel down. Unique numbers, special attention.

11 – idealistic, visionary, inspiring as a teacher, highly sensitive, a great spiritual teacher, intuitive, perfectionist

22 – vibration of 4 raised to an even higher level, lover of world peace, ambitious, excellent common sense,

organised, master builder, visionary with their feet on the ground

**33 – Christ Consciousness**

## According to the Tarot

### The Aces (1)

Beginnings, an idea, an action, or venture. Being an individual.

### The Twos

Becoming two, joining together in partnerships, both intimate and platonic. Sharing warmth, loving, friendly peace-making number. Harmony, olive branches, rifts healed and reconciliations.

### The Threes

Enjoyment of life and being outgoing and gregarious. Intellect, growth and abundance. People are fun-loving, charming, entertaining, show-offs yet sensitive.

### The Fours

Four is the number of material completion. Stability of spirit, intellect, emotion and material life. Balance and harmonious. Be careful not to become too rigid or get bogged down in material matters.

People will be reliable, practical, diligent, patient, insistent on detail, accurate, hard-working, self-disciplined and sincere, they work well in the business world, and with finance, but show few artistic or creative urges.

### The Fives

Five is severe conflict and strife. It shows difficulties and upheaval. The number 5 is associated with the planet Mars, so powerful, dramatic, often bringing quarrels and anger. However, it shows courage and passion, often coming out on top.

## The Sixes

Six is a lovely number, the number of family and generosity. Charity is often linked to the number 6 and you can trust that if it relates to a person, then they will be kind, helpful and trustworthy. Number 6 people are peacemakers, well-rounded and balanced.

You'll remember that 3's were about the completion of a stage. Later, you will see that 9's are about ultimate completion. The number 6 lies in the middle between these two numbers, therefore halfway along the way to ultimate completion. Merging is an important principle connected with 6, it is a point of balance.

## The Sevens

Seven to me is a number, and for thousands of years in many traditions, it has been called a 'lucky' number. There are seven colours in a rainbow, seven original planets used in astrology, and not forgetting, the seven veils of existence, seven days of the week, and in Buddhism there are the seven steps of ascension into Godhead. So, it holds much spiritual significance.

Seven is the pillars of wisdom and relates to the personal growth of understanding and knowledge within the individual.

## The Eights

The number eight is a number that is drawn with two circles, two completed circles, therefore the number eight refers to a completion of some sort. In the Major Arcana, The Magician card has the infinity symbol above his head, this looks very much like a number eight on its side, which looks like a figure eight lying on its side. This is one of the symbols for infinity; the glyph or symbol is indicating perfect balance of forces. Eights are concerned with practical matters too, like the number four, but the strength is doubled. Hard work and attention to detail is indicated and the saying, 'to reap, we must sow.'

## The Nines

The number 9 allows us to see the rewards of our labours and whatever we have been working towards is coming to fruition.

This wonderful number corresponds with the colour of gold, in fact it is linked to teachers and healers, and it is often said and seen that people who heal have gold in their auras. I find it amazing that I was born on the 9th of September (9th month) and am both a teacher (primary, special needs and now spiritual) and a healer!

We also associate gold with riches and wealth.

## The Tens

This number sums up our thoughts, actions, plans and, even, our mistakes. It is about the recognition that you have completed a stage in your life and that you have now manifested exactly what you have been aiming for.

The number 10 is of completion in the nought, and with the 1 we start again. So, it is the end of one phase and the beginning of another.

# Chapter 18

# Angel Numbers

I do this little connection exercise when I am driving: I look out and ask for 'Angel' numbers. Like the meanings of each number in numerology, angels can communicate with us through the patterns of numbers. When you see recurring patterns of the same number, it holds a higher vibration, an angelic vibration. Below is an overview of what each recurring angelic number means, however, I have adapted my numbers (or some of them) to link with personal people in my life. When I see those numbers, I smile as I know that special person is with me. For example, 666 is a family, affectionate, healing and nurturing number and this reminds me of my nan. 999 has a spiritual connection, it also is the date of my dad's and my birthday, so when I see 999, I know my dad is with me.

My nan had an affinity with the number 6. All through her life, positive things happened on the 6th, or dates that added to 6, or had a 6 in it like the number 26th (my mum's birthday) and 16 (my aunt's birthday). So naturally, every time I see 666, I know my nan is around.

There is no right or wrong way to use numbers. I hope you understand through reading this book, that I believe everything is down to intuition and own interpretation, and it is important you believe what is right for you. Trust your inner guidance, your Higher Self, your intuition.

## Angelic Numbers

**111** – Opportunities are opening for you. Watch your thoughts as they are manifesting.

**222** – One becomes 2, partnerships. The coming together either through a partnership (romantic or business) or a situation is resolving itself.

**333** – The Ascended Masters are near you, know that you have their help, love and companionship. In this moment, sense which Ascended Master it is, and it will be the one that first springs into your mind.

**444** – The number of angels, they are surrounding you at this moment, giving you love and support.*

**555** – A major life change is upon you. This is positive even though it may not feel like it at the time. Change involves stepping out of your comfort zone, breaking through the barriers and stepping into your light.

**666** – Your thoughts are out of balance right now. Maybe you are focusing too much on the material world. This number pattern brings harmony and comfort.

**777** – A spiritual and magical number, it is a reminder to keep up the good work and know that your wishes are coming true.

**888** – The meaning of this pattern shows us the light at the end of the tunnel. It is about foundation, prosperity and security.

**999** – Another spiritual number. It signifies that you are a light worker. The world needs you right now.

**000** – A reminder that you are at one with God. It is also a sign that a situation has come full circle.

---

* I saw this number as I rushed to the hospital to see my dad after he had a heart attack and collapsed in the car whilst driving. I have to say I was both angry at seeing it and comforted at the same time. I knew he was with the angels before I arrived at the hospital, even though I begged them not to take him. The loss of someone close still affects you even when you are a medium and totally believe in the afterlife and how it works. We are human and will always miss the physical person and prefer them to be with us here on Earth.

# Chapter 19

# Working with the Moon

Before I was guided into mediumship, I felt an incredibly strong pull toward astrology. I read book after book, absorbing as much information that I could. I loved the fact that we are born on a specific day, in a specific month, in a specific year and that it all tied into the place of our birth and how the planets aligned, which created our individual character. This blew my mind and I researched everyone around me to see what they were like, whether we were compatible and how we connected. Unfortunately to become an astrologer, there was learning to draw charts, understanding the planets (which I did learn), and all manner of other complicated things, that I didn't take it further. I realise now that I simply needed to understand the basics to support my mediumship and I often, in fact always, get given suns or planets to support my evidence, so the hard work in my teens really paid off.

## Working with the moon

Since a young girl I have had an affinity with the moon. I religiously watched her phases as she grew and shrank. I love the bright, mesmerising full moon and the slight crescent, and yes, I used to think people lived on the moon but laughed at the idea it was made from cheese – I wasn't that daft! I used to follow it around the sky and wonder why it kept moving too and intuitively spoke to the 'moon' although I wasn't sure why or who I was communicating and off-loading to. Fast forward in time, I began studying astrology, reading everything I could find and constantly checked my horoscopes to see what life was bringing me or to understand why I felt the way I did. I found out not only my sun sign, but what my rising sign was and where in my astrological cycle I could find my moon. I found it in the sign of Gemini.

It was later, in my late teens/early twenties, when I started on the discovery that the moon with its cyclical journey fell in line with my menstrual cycle, and the moon's phases flowed and ebbed causing my emotions to follow suit. I noticed that I am overwhelmed and emotional at the full moon, yet positive and energised at the new moon.

Over the years I have taken several courses to help me understand the moon who I fondly recognise as 'The Divine Feminine'. I can wholeheartedly recommend *Moonology* by Yasmin Boland. She has helped me to work with the moon in various ways to connect with her energies and to work alongside her gifts to support my emotional, spiritual and working life. The moon phases speak to me daily and her interaction with the planets and star signs has become a bible for me to understand myself at a deeper level.

Working with the moon phases is really simple. It can get complex but I believe in simplicity so have broken the moon's teachings down in a way which is accessible to me and to you. Firstly, each full moon has a name, some of which originate through traditions from different cultures here in the UK and throughout the world. Whereby these names are not astrological, they were originally used by farmers, shepherds, Native American tribes to name a few. You will see two lists as the moon names hold different meanings according to the hemisphere you live in.

### Northern Hemisphere
January – Wolf Moon
February – Snow Moon
March – Worm Moon
April – Pink Moon
May – Flower Moon

June – Strawberry Moon
July – Buck Moon
August – Sturgeon Moon
September – Harvest Moon
October – Hunter's Moon
November – Beaver Moon
December – Cold Moon

## Southern Hemisphere

January – Buck Moon
February – Sturgeon Moon
March – Harvest Moon
April – Hunter's Moon
May – Beaver Moon
June – Cold Moon
July – Wolf Moon
August – Snow Moon
September – Worm Moon
October – Pink Moon
November – Flower Moon
December – Strawberry Moon

You will notice a theme to why these moons are named thus: usually an indication of what is happening during that month and this helped the people to understand time and seasons throughout the year.

Supermoons occur when the moon is at the closest point to the Earth during her orbit. Her actual size doesn't change. However, because she is closer, she appears bigger and brighter. During the Supermoon and because the moon is closer, it has an increased effect on the gravity of the Earth, affecting the tides. Our bodies are made up of approximately 70% water, therefore we may feel super emotional and it could play with our physical and mental states. You may also find that you are more intuitive around this time and possibly more sensitive.

## Phases of the Moon

There are eight phases of the moon, and as she travels through them, you will notice how she changes shape. This is because the moon doesn't have its own light, it is reflected light from the sun, so depending on where the sun is will make it appear like it is increasing (waxing) or decreasing (waning) in size.

I have detailed what energy corresponds with each moon phase along with an image to support visual understanding. This is a brief outline because the topic of the moon is so vast and in-depth that it really can only be comprehended through lots of study and I can't honour that here.

Once again, please bear in mind that the moon appears different depending on which hemisphere you live in.

## Diagram of the phases of the moon

New Moon – This is a beautiful phase of the moon which will be perfect for planting your seeds of dreams and desires. It signifies potential, new beginnings, growth and excitement.

Waxing – During this amazing period, explore dreams fully and remember to hold your faith as you have set your dreams in motion by expressing them under the New Moon.

First Quarter Moon – As we enter this phase, we may come across some challenges or our faith may be tested in some way. So continue your commitment and hold your desires firmly in your mind, beaming confidence and positivity towards them.

Gibbous Moon – Time to have a rethink about your hopes, plans and desired outcomes that you set during your New Moon wishes. If you feel that there needs to be some tweaking, or adjustments, now, under the Gibbous Moon, is the perfect time to do this.

Full Moon – As the glorious light of the Full Moon shines brightly, evaluate how far you have come and give gratitude for all you have or what you have achieved already. See any results coming to fruition and welcome them. Now is a wonderful opportunity to let go of what doesn't serve you or your pathway, and release them with love to the Full Moon. Graciously, give forgiveness to yourself or others so that you are not holding any lower emotions or energy in your space. Send yourself or others love and good intentions – remember you are not saying it is OK to be hurt or treated badly, but you are no longer willing to hold that negative energy in your aura or within your heart.

Disseminating Moon – Breathe and relax, there is nothing better than to give yourself some loving time under this very important phase of the moon. Walk in nature, go outdoor swimming, anything which brings joy and relaxation.

Third Quarter Moon – This period is another opportunity for you to re-evaluate your plans. Do they still feel right? What is preventing them flowing in the right direction? What can you do to support, change, realign your journey to reach your desired outcome? Then make sure you balance your emotions to give you the strength to fulfil any tasks which need to be completed.

Balsamic Moon – During this period, spend time releasing your fears, healing your emotions and surrendering to the abundant, magical and loving Divine Feminine energy of the Moon.

## Full Moon

The Full Moon is a very powerful time, she illuminates areas or situations in our lives which we need to release because they are no longer serving us. This could be people, work but also negative thought patterns. Often, we get trapped in our recurring thoughts, negative thoughts about ourselves which only escalate under the Full Moon.

To help you feel less emotional, try to focus solely on things which only serve your highest and greatest good. Release people, fears, situations or past memories which are holding you back from moving forward. Practise the gift of 'Forgiveness'. Forgiving people releases you of the bind that keeps you in that moment. When someone has behaved badly or inappropriately to you, you are forever stuck in the negative emotions, and each time you think about them or the situation, you relive the scenario, hear the words all over again and feel the emotion flooding through your soul. This prevents you from moving on in peace and harmony, so under the Full Moon, state that:

I forgive... for... and I release you into the light of the moon. I welcome love and healing to my thoughts and know that I am healed.

The Full Moon is also a great time to forgive yourself for any wrongdoings you have consciously or unconsciously done to others and forgive yourself for any negative thoughts or comments you have directed at yourself – we all say detrimental things about ourselves, which we shouldn't as the vibrations of these words penetrate our energy, and if we don't catch them, they will begin to turn into our core beliefs.

Treating ourselves with a cleansing salt bath, or a crystal bath, with candles and incense during the Full Moon can be a beautiful experience. It helps to empty our mind and aura of any residual lower energy we have collected up during the month and helps to recharge our batteries. We can do the same for our crystals to cleanse them in any way we feel drawn to and then place them in the light of the Full Moon (inside or outside).

You can use the Full Moon too to celebrate your successes, congratulate yourself on how far you have come already!

Rituals are an amazing way to connect with your innermost desires and can be a powerful way to help you amplify your intentions. Creating these rituals during the powerful New and Full Moons will make them even stronger. I have written two rituals which I use. They are simple and easy to perform, however, as usual, make them your own, follow your intuition and personalise them.

## Full Moon Ritual

- ° Play some calming music, light a candle, hold your crystals.
- ° Connect with your breath.
- ° Think of all the things, people, situations which no longer serve you and you wish to release.
- ° Go through them separately and visualise them, feel them.
- ° Then write them down in order on a piece of paper.
- ° Burn them safely in the candle flame for transmutation into love.
- ° Feel them releasing from you as they burn, notice yourself becoming lighter.

- State your forgiveness.
- State, "I am healed of these limiting thoughts and emotions for my highest and greatest good. I am love."

## New Moon

The New Moon is a marvellous time to kick-start a new project, to set intentions for what you wish to achieve or plan to do. It is about manifesting your desires and helping you to jumpstart your plans. This could be love, a home move, a new job or the success of a project. It can be anything you have dreamt of, think big, but as always, the success of these dreams coming to fruition will totally depend on if it is for your highest and greatest good. I did say think big, but bear in mind, you may need to organise your goal into baby steps.

The New Moon is also a time for growth, blessings and healing. Use this phase to reflect on your blessings and give thanks.

### New Moon Ritual

- Light a candle, play some calming music, light some incense.
- Breathe and ground your energy.
- Give thanks for your blessings.
- Visualise your New Moon wishes or desires – be clear and specific.
- Meditate on them as if they have already happened and you are living your dream. Notice how good you feel.
- Write them down and keep them safe.
- State that they are for your highest and greatest good.
- Give thanks to the Moon.

*Once your wishes have been written down, you can use the other phases of the moon through the month to reflect, adjust or add to them.*

Sometimes life gets so busy and we find it hard to set aside a space for ourselves, so even if you haven't the time to treat yourself to a New or Full Moon ritual, then you can do these two simple, quick yet effective practices.

## Full Moon:

- Go outside if possible, or look at the moon through an open window.
- Light a candle or incense stick (or both).
- Give thanks for all you have which is positive.
- Say an affirmation to clear, cleanse, or let go of something which is holding you back.
- Say a forgiveness prayer.
- If you have written these down and it is safe to do, burn it.
- Say, "Thank You."

## New Moon:

- Go outside if possible, or look at the moon through an open window.
- Light a candle or incense stick (or both).
- Give gratitude for all you have.
- Meditate on all your desires you wish to draw towards you.
- Visualise them as if you have already achieved them, feel the emotion.
- Give thanks to the New Moon.

## Meditation

- Ground
- Connect with the energy of the moon
- Feel her vibration
- Allow her light to flood and infuse you
- Get brighter and bright

- Flow
- Affirm
- Gratitude

## Crystals Associated with the Moon

*Full Moon* – crystals to bring peace, forgiveness, harmony, healing
Selenite
White Howlite
Aquamarine

*New Moon* – crystals for protection, grounding, dispelling negativity, removing blockages
Black Tourmaline
Black Obsidian
Haematite

However you wish to use the moon's energy, simply being aware of the cycles and your emotions will help transform your daily life and decision making. I chose the crescent moon in Virgo to send this book off to the publishers!

# Chapter 20

# Past Lives and Their Importance

It was about seven years ago that I became interested in past life regression seriously. Before I was a little scared in case I found out that I was somebody horrible or that something nasty had happened to me. I was also worried about going under hypnosis. Believing there was an afterlife and knowing that when we passed over, we would eventually come back as someone else, reincarnate, I knew that I needed to explore this path and learn how it works and what happens. My journey into past life regression was amazing; it really resonated with me and now I use it with people to help them understand why they do some of the things they do, to help them understand reoccurring issues and to bring about the release or healing. Past life regression is very powerful; it's not just an exercise to be nosey at what other lives you have lived – although that's fun too.

Our soul is our essence, it's the pure aspect of ourselves, it is all that we are. We are made up of Spirit, our consciousness and our body, the home we are living in for this incarnation. Our soul's journey is what we look at when we investigate our past lives, it is who we are as a whole because every life we have chosen, and it was our choice, has helped us to grow and develop and we will continue to grow and develop until we have learnt everything our soul needs to learn. While meeting with a team of light – the council, made up of angels, guides and souls who assist you in planning your next incarnation during your life-between-life – you outline together how your soul will grow and ascend. At this meeting we make our 'Soul Contract' with the other souls stepping in to volunteer joining you for your earthly incarnation. It may be decided that they either help you learn your toughest lessons or indeed will support you through it. Through this meeting you will identify and address your karma, weaving together your life plan and purpose. There are no coincidences, everything significant is planned even down to your date of birth and the country you live in. Once everything has been decided, you are given your gifts. These are gifts to help you manage your life, for instance, strength or patience, but also to support your soul's mission. An entrepreneur is creative, passionate, hardworking, a nurse is caring, patient, loving, and a policeman is brave, quick thinking.

Each time we incarnate and come to Earth with our soul mission plan, we have in our blueprint a loosely laid-out map of certain events that will steer our path and bring knowledge, understanding and experiences. I say loosely because we have free will and there are many pathways we can choose to follow. The overall journey is planned, so marriage/relationships, children, particular jobs, homes etc are all events we have chosen up in the 'drawing board' as I call it, and these events will be based on the type of learning our souls need. For example, your soul may wish to experience poverty, to feel what it is like not to have a safe home, regular meals, clean water to drink. Your soul may have already experienced a wealthy life and need to balance it with poverty so that, overall, you understand the importance of necessity in life. I talked about having a shadow side, well this is similar. How can you appreciate money if you have always had it? Surely then you would take it for granted and be frivolous. If you experience poverty, then it balances out the other life experiences and your soul can grow. It is often said that we grow from hardship.

Choosing a difficult life may sound lonely or scary but you have help. In the 'Planning Room' there are higher vibrational souls, your soul family, which you have incarnated many, many, many times with before, and your Guardian Angel. Together they offer to join you to help you grow, teach you the lessons your soul needs to expand through or to support you through the specific life. These souls may incarnate around the same time, but sometimes they will need to go first (parents, grandparents, older people you meet, or join you later e.g., children), but they always volunteer to do so. These members of your soul family will also have their own lessons to learn, lessons to expand their soul, so the whole process gets drafted out and planned perfectly with Divine Timing. The right country, area, social setting, your parents and family, the day and time you are born (linking back to astrology for the traits and characters needed to steer you in that life), and other factors necessary to support the journey.

You will know when you are with a member of your soul family because they will feel familiar to you. I have always had a deep connection with my mum, my aunt and my cousin. I feel that they truly understand me, and we are very alike. The emotions between us go deeper than any other connection. I have a wonderful family and am very close to my sister (and my dad in spirit), but the energy is different.

When I met my husband, I knew within a couple of hours that I would marry him. We just clicked and connected, and when we left the restaurant where we were having a dinner with his university friends (I worked with one of the girls which was why I was there, I knew nobody else) we walked outside to a club. It was a short distance, and without knowing, we held hands. I knew then. It was like finding something which you had been looking for but had to wait until the timing was right. I believe my husband, like the others I mentioned above, is one of my soul mates, from my soul family. However, it is important to note that not all soul relationships are perfect like in the films. A soul mate can be your biggest teacher and the relationship may not always be easy.

When you are ready to return to Earth, you will be assigned a Guardian Angel and a Guide (or several guides depending on your soul mission). Together they will support and help you navigate your life as planned. Think of a friend holding a map. If you steer off too far, they will pull you back, nudge you and send out signs so that you pay attention. Consider now all those times when you feel things are wrong, situations, places, people. When you are in the wrong job, your Guardian Angel and Guides (you will be assigned one, but many others will come and go to help you along the way and teach you) will orchestrate scenarios to help you make changes. You may have a terrible boss; you may experience difficulties in the workplace and eventually decide to leave. It is only when you are following your soul path, that you feel happy, centred, true to yourself. Once again this is my understanding and I encourage you to explore these words yourself; sit with your angels and guides and ask them.

## What Is Your Soul?

Your soul is the infinite part of you which has been evolving over many lifetimes, it is a spark of the Divine which needs a body to help it grow spiritually. The body is a vessel which the soul has chosen for this current lifetime. The soul only wants what is best for us, it holds our blueprint, our map, and its message to us is simply that it wants us to know that it is always there, guiding us, offering love and support. The soul's language is communicated to us through signs, synchronicity and intuition. If we choose not to listen, the messages will only get louder. So what is your soul trying to whisper to you? First, we have to step out of our body (ego) and let our soul speak to us.

Sometimes our body and soul aren't always in alignment. We can be at odds with ourselves – the heart (soul) and the mind (body). When our emotions and actions are acting out of the ego, we will feel anger, hate, greed or jealousy, however, the soul only feels love and compassion. Give yourself time to listen, allow your light to glow and remember the soul guides you to your passions because this allows your soul to expand.

Your body and soul are in partnership – we (ego) might want things to happen, but allow the soul (heart) to tell you what it needs. When we listen, doors will open, opportunities will present themselves and the right people will introduce themselves.

## Can You Heal Your Soul?

Yes, definitely.

We have had many lifetimes, some have dimmed our light through difficulty, pain and trauma, whereas others have expanded our soul, lifting us up. To understand our true soul mission, we must first clear past karmic lessons which we no longer need to experience, releasing them, cutting them loose and finding the understanding within them. We must sever those karmic ties that we no longer require. These are the patterns we keep learning and experiencing which are holding us back and preventing soul growth.

However, it is not just our own lessons we are learning; remember we also have family and ancestral karmic lessons, even karmic ties to places.

Why is it that we are born in certain places or move to certain places which draw us? Why are there certain people who we intuitively feel bonded with? It is because these souls have agreed to join us on this life mission so that they can either help and support us, guide us or indeed teach us. The teaching may sometimes feel difficult and hurtful, but to grow, we must fall. On the other hand, beautiful connections are made to welcome in new souls (children) or encourage our soul to learn, to grow to experience love.

Amongst us are truly amazing souls who have answered the call from the Universe to help our planet, to understand and encourage others, physically, emotionally, mentally and spiritually. Awakening them. These Earth Angels are special and radiate the brightest of lights.

In order to align with our essence and see our true colour, the colour of our soul, and truly shine, we need to heal the karmic ties that no longer serve us.

## Past Life Regression

What it is past life regression? As I explained above, we will have many, many, many different incarnations (please don't think about these in terms of a linear line because time and space are interwoven, and we are living our lives at once), and all these experiences make us who we are and who we will become. In every life we bring an essence with us, a spark of energy as we do not bring our whole soul down; our soul is having other life experiences as there are many tiny sparks breaking away from our huge soul. Don't worry, they all come back!

In each life we bring back some of the energy we have already experienced. Staying with the same theme of poverty, if we had a life where we lived in a small fishing village in a tiny hut and the only food we could eat was what we fished or grew, then in this life we may experience a love of the sea, living off the land or alternatively you may have had so many fish that it has caused a negative reaction and you hate the smell and taste of fish. Where do find all these memories? There are many different terms. The Akashic Records – described as a complete universal record of every thought, deed, action and emotion that has ever occurred or ever will occur. It is often described as The Book of Records, The Higher Self – the greater part of ourselves which we can access to gain knowledge and wisdom (our intuition) to help guide and protect us through our life's journey and The Soul – our essence of who we are and includes our intellect, will, emotions, conscious, heart and mind. Our soul is eternal and exists beyond our physical life and body. Our memories are held in the mind known as our subconscious.

If you are interested in this, please read around the subject or have a past life regression to experience it first-hand because this topic really does need a whole book to explain it thoroughly.

Recalling past lives can be done with a therapist who will use hypnosis to take you into a deep state of meditation. This is important, as during this state, your conscious mind is turned down (it will never be switched off), so that you can tap into the subconscious, where our memories of all that we have and all that will be are homed. From here, the therapist will guide you through one or several past lives and help you achieve what you need to understand. I will mention more about how past life regression can help you later.

Remembering past lives can also be triggered spontaneously. Maybe you have visited a place and can remember it clearly or know deep within your being that you have lived there. An obsession with a period of history, like I have with Ancient Egypt and the Tudors, can be a sign that you have lived in that period. There have been some wonderful stories of children who have remembered past lives where they say, "I was your mum in another life." Dreams can also signify memories of other lives.

It doesn't matter why you would wish to have a past life regression. As I said before, it may be simple nosiness, but it can bring healing, healing for this life and also a past life, especially if there are issues you are facing in your current life. Understanding where certain characteristics or traits come from if they cannot be understood within your family or due to experiences you have had in your current life e.g., trauma, then looking at past lives can help you. When I regress a client, I usually take them through at least three different lives. I do this because we get to see a common pattern or find reasons why an issue is causing you difficulties. When we arrive in what is known as 'between lives', where you have experienced a passing, you can be guided to review that said life and the issues held there. I guide you with questions like, what have you learnt from that specific life and what understanding you can bring into your present life. This part of the regression is also brilliant and important for any healing to take place such as forgiveness (yourself and others) so that you can release the emotions attached to the event and therefore release it from your current life.

With a recommended therapist, past life regression can be a wonderful experience. You can find recorded ones which are great, but they will not be able to guide you specifically, so you probably won't get to solve any deep-seated emotions. During the regressions I have conducted, I have been lucky enough to witness some amazing past lives. One experience helped me to understand a bigger picture, which I've shared below.

### Account from Etain
*I have no feet. I am a swan; I can see my feathers and I am on a lake in a garden of a big house. I am a male swan and there are other swans around me, but I am in charge! I am searching for food.*

*I have a pain in my neck, I have been hit on the neck with sticks that the boys are holding. They hit me when I flared my wings at them trying to protect my female. They hit me on the back of the neck and I'm really in pain. I have my babies and I just wanted to protect them and my female. They hit me on the back of the head, my head is falling down, I'm crying.*

*(Few days later – seconds in the PLR) I'm dead! I see the foxes eat me – I never felt it. I'm floating somewhere, not flying but floating. It is bright white, calm, happy and peaceful. I am not in the sky or water, just floating around in nothing, gently floating around.*

*I like the light, it's beautiful, shiny and white. Big ball of light.*

*I am going into a tunnel. I want to stay here; something is pulling me but I want to stay.*

This past life regression not only highlighted that we are souls who can incarnate many times, but sometimes as animals. I asked my guides how this can happen and I was told that whatever your soul needs to learn or experience, you can choose the 'story'. Here, Etain needed to understand about protection and how life can be short, so a swan was a perfect choice. It was a quick life but she now holds in her cell memory the knowledge of standing up for others, protection of family and consequences.

I love that during this regression, we see her soul floating up to 'Heaven' or the place we go home, which helps us to understand both the amazing feelings of serenity, tranquillity, and love, but also that even the animal kingdom return home to Source.

## Chapter 21

# Meditation and Sitting in the Power

I will cover the many benefits and the different types of meditation deeper in Part Three. However, I must mention now how meditation can help you understand yourself. This practice connects you to your Higher Self, and through this connection, you will receive guidance for the situations in your present life.

Every living thing has a unique spirit, this includes plants, animals and humans. By spirit I mean character, personality, beliefs etc and to begin to understand others you need to begin to understand yourself. Recognising and discovering your own spirit is an important first step as it will help you to understand who you are, and from that starting point, you can begin to understand and help others, becoming less judgemental as you learn to understand that we are all different, make different choices, based on our personal experiences, and will evolve at different rates which are in line with our soul development.

Understanding ourselves as I said in the beginning of this book can be uncomfortable. It is about being honest with ourselves, which can be hard, but it is also wonderful when you realise that our own qualities aren't bad, but they may be holding us back. For example, being shy or nervous doesn't make you a nasty person, but it will prevent you from achieving certain goals which may include standing up in front of an audience to give a presentation. Looking deeply at your traits you will also discover your strengths, the positives that make people love, respect or admire you. This exercise will help you to find out what makes you tick, the patterns you keep following, and through this process you will get a sense of empathy for yourself too. Remember always being gentle on yourself; this is not about picking holes, it is about blending with yourself.

Once we learn more about ourselves and find out what makes us feel complete, what feeds our spirit bringing us contentment, the more we will begin to like ourselves. Once we believe we are OK, decent, even likable and loveable, our senses will come alive. We can identify with what inspires and drives us and then we can truly feed our spirit and the growing can begin, because unfortunately a spirit that is not fed cannot grow spiritually. To be our true spiritual self, we must understand ourselves, our whole self and iron out the creases, releasing anything and anyone that doesn't feed us joy, that no longer serves us.

This is where meditation comes into the fore. Many people question meditation, but it is the perfect time to understand yourself. A regular meditation practice is a vital part of growing spiritually and developing your psychic and mediumship gift. It will take time, but slowly and eventually with practice you will be able to do the meditations naturally. There are many ways to meditate which I will discuss later, but in terms of understanding yourself it is important to listen to your Higher Self. Our Higher Self offers us guidance in our everyday lives. It knows the best outcomes to take for any situation and it is the 'best' part of us, the part that is good, compassionate, caring, empathic, sensitive, loyal, kind and non-judgemental. It helps us to move through our fears and anxieties. Wouldn't you listen to that? Meditation is the perfect way to connect you to your Higher Self.

### Exercise to Connect with Your Higher Self

Centre yourself with breathing.

Connect in with your breath, slow steady breaths, in and out.

Send your roots into Mother Earth, really grounding yourself.

Bring down the white light of Spirit through each chakra.

Expand the white light into your aura.

Affirm that you are ready to connect with your Higher Self for communication, for your highest and greatest good.

See or feel a beautiful golden light surrounding you.

Connect, then listen.

Welcome any images, colours, words but don't try to analyse them. Simply accept the wisdom they bring.

Sit in this altered state for as long as you wish (between 10-20 minutes).

Give thanks for the knowledge and guidance.

# Chapter 22

# Protection

As with all types of work, we need to protect ourselves and the best protection has been given to us by Archangel Michael. I have used this short but very effective visualisation many, many times and it has always proven to work. However, what you do have to remember though, is that there is a higher order, a great life plan, and so if something is meant to happen it will as it will be for either our highest and greatest good or an initiation that we have agreed to undergo for our learning, development or for karmic reasons.

Surrounding yourself with protection is a way of guarding your energy so you are not drained or pulled down energetically. If this is happening to you (and it can be unconsciously done by another), then below are some quick and simple ways to protect yourself.

- Say the Lord's Prayer.
- Call upon Archangel Michael's bubble of protection – see below.
- Imagine mirrors surrounding you, reflecting back the negativity but again ask it to be returned as love.
- Call upon your Guardian Angels and guides to surround you in their loving and protective energy.
- Call upon Mother Mary.
- Use crystals such as black tourmaline, obsidian, haematite, onyx, jet, smoky quartz etc to absorb negative energy and crystals such as rose quartz, sunstone, green aventurine or blue lace agate etc which radiate love, understanding and calm.
- Recite affirmations of protection.

It is important to note that before you protect yourself, you need to be clear of any residual negativity you may be holding on to otherwise you are simply locking in your energy and amplifying it. These are just some of my ways to cleanse my energy.

**To cleanse your energy**

- ☐ Smudge using incense e.g., sage
- ☐ Use the white light of Spirit
- ☐ Sound – drums, bells, tingsha cymbals, tuning forks
- ☐ Crystals – especially selenite brushing
- ☐ Grounding techniques
- ☐ Intention – set your intentions for being protected and energetically safe
- ☐ Essential oils – e.g., frankincense
- ☐ Water – bathing, streams
- ☐ Moon bathing
- ☐ Mantra and positive affirmations

Remember too that you alone are in control of your energy, it is yours to hold onto or give away. Being disciplined with the company you keep can be beneficial. However, if it is family then make sure you follow the steps above and you will soon notice how their mindsets will change for the better.

### Archangel Michael's Bubble of Protection
*Ask Archangel Michael to surround you in a bubble of protection, visualise this and ask that only love, light and goodness can filter through. Ask that any negativity be sent back to where it came from as love. Say thanks.*

Another way to use the help of Archangel Michael is to visualise a royal blue cloak of protection covering you all the way from your head to your feet. Know that you are safe.

Also, at night time or in public places, pull your aura in towards your body. This way you are not so open and will not get drained by other people's energy. Unfortunately, public places are filled with energy, some wonderful and giving, some not as much. Sadness, grief, trauma, anger and resentment can fill our auras if we are going through difficult times. We don't want to be walking through this, so pulling in our auras will help us escape it and keep our own energy clear and balanced.

## Other Tips to Protect Yourself or Clear the Energy around You

○ Cleanse your room with sage with the intent of clearing negative energy, then open the window to allow the old energy out. Visualise this happening.

○ Place rose quartzes in the four corners of your room to keep the energy loving and pure. Keep a selenite in there too and a black obsidian. Cleanse the crystals regularly, but do not use water with the selenite, use sage, a Palo Santo incense stick or whatever you are drawn to use.

○ Visualise a white light coming down through your chakras, cleansing your energy as it goes down (coffee plunger). See the old energy going into the ground and then turning into green grass or flowers (something positive).

○ If the protection is from spirits who pop up to communicate with you when you are not ready to work then state your intentions to Spirit. Be precise when and how you want to work; you set the rules.

People often ask me about ghosts and what is the difference between ghosts and spirits. My understanding is that ghosts are residual energy; they are attached to a place or building where they either died or hold a memory. By this I mean that their death may have been traumatic, violent, or heartbreaking.

Due to this, they either chose not to pass over into the light or they refused to believe they were dead, therefore leaving them trapped. Often you will see ghosts tracing the steps of the final stages of life or repeatedly following a daily routine. Many people have reported seeing ghosts walk through a wall. Well, it could just be that when they were alive there used to be a door, or that the building that the observer is in wasn't there 100 years ago.

My aunt has a ghost (well many) in her house, but this one belongs to the land, not the house, even though he is drawn to her energy and the energy of her family. Her house was built on a piece of land belonging to The Netherlands; hence her road being called Netherlands Road.

Usually a ghost will be 'looking' for something and refuse to leave until they find it. These ghosts are not harmful, they will not know you are there and they will not interfere. They don't haunt people or places in a negative sense; however, some find it disturbing. The ghosts which haunt are what I call spirit, but spirit who have chosen not to go into the light or the afterlife and I will break this down into easy terms for you, due to my understanding.

There are two types of spirit; the first type are our loved ones, our family members, friends, pets and colleagues. These spirits have left their earthly bodies and have chosen to face their fate, realising that this was the Divine plan and it was their time to go home. In returning home, they receive healing, piece together what they have learnt according to their life mission and how their actions, thoughts and deeds have sculpted their ascension and karmic lessons. These beautiful spirits come back to visit us. Initially they stay around us to make sure we are coping with their death, to give us comfort and warmth, reassurance, healing and love. Later, as time passes, they begin to guide and support us in our daily lives. They can help us understand why they were like they were or help us to see a clearer picture of what we need to do. This can be easily understood by yourself through meditation, signs or whispers, but for less sensitive people, through a medium. These types of spirits, our loved ones, only hold love for us, want forgiveness and bring positive messages of hope.

The second type of spirits are those which have not crossed over due to unsettling circumstances such as trauma or tragedy. They are so-called 'trapped' between two existences. They may or may not know they are dead but mostly don't want to move on as they are waiting for a loved one to join them or they may want to find out what happened to them. Maybe they loved their home and are happy staying there and, in some circumstances I have heard about, they are frightened to pass over as they may not have been a 'good' person in life and are worried what the afterlife may have in store for them. This is particularly true of those who are religious and believe in the Devil and Hell. I want to communicate with them all and reassure them that this, in my opinion, isn't true. God is love, we are his children and why would someone hurt their child. Yes, there are consequences, yes, we need to be held responsible for our choices we made and yes there will be karmic lessons to balance, but punishment, I don't believe so. It's not my understanding and I believe when we pass into the afterlife, we see how our choices have affected our ascension and then our new life plan will be adjusted accordingly.

So, spirits which 'haunt' are stuck energies which probably have been negative in their earthly body. They may have been troublemakers, violent, aggressive, or simply stubborn. My aunt's spirits, which are very happy living side by side with her and the family, get a little irksome when they make changes to the house, decorate or when lots of people (other energies) enter what they view is their space. She has known glass vases to smash, beds to vibrate, things to go missing, being locked out of her own house and electric items going wrong. Not harmful but irritating, nonetheless.

Some spirits want to be noticed. They want to warn you away from 'their' home or wish to grab your attention. Attention-seeking spirits will band, knock, lock, move, tamper with electrical things e.g., lights, radios, give cold spots or allow themselves to be seen. The more you are scared, the more they draw from your energy. An aggressive spirit will provoke the kind of emotion that intensifies fear to gain energy. They may even drain enough energy from you that they can move things – you may have heard of poltergeists. These spirits can be harmful, if not physically then emotionally, however, they can only be so if you provide them the energy. In these circumstances, protection and spirit release may be needed.

### Emma's story

*Emma is a teenager and granddaughter of a friend. Her grandmother contacted me to ask for some advice as her granddaughter had been having some strange occurrences. She had begun to feel a heavy energy in her bedroom and caught a glimpse of a dark shadowy person on several occasions which naturally scared her. Although nothing had happened, she felt threatened and believed the energy was evil.*

*I spoke with Emma, and as she told me the events, I linked into the energy, and believed that although it felt scary, he was not harmful. Emma is in her late teens and this can be the time when spirit can make themselves known. It happened to me, although I was younger. Teenagers are going through many hormone changes and it is a time when they feel unsure, anxious and vulnerable. Spirits, particularly those with a lower energy, are attracted to the energy of teenagers, they draw from it and it makes them more powerful. I am talking poltergeists here, lower spirit energy that use our energy to move, throw, smash objects. Emma's spirit presence wasn't a poltergeist, just an elderly man who lived in the house before her family was there. Emma is psychic like her grandmother. Her own energy, known as her aura, glowed like a beacon which was what* spirit was after. As Emma had no experience of spiritual things, it all seemed strange and dark.

Emma wanted me to perform a spirit release, but because I lived so far away, I couldn't do one for her. Instead, I asked her to use selenite, a white gypsum which is a powerful crystal that transmutes lower energy, clearing it to raise the vibration of the person and the room. I also asked her to light some candles, white but not necessarily, to again change the energy in the room. I talked her through a protection visualisation where she called upon Archangel Michael to place a protective bubble around herself allowing only love and goodness to enter and to bounce back any negativity, but as LOVE. This is important as we do not want to become like those who send negative energy in the form of thoughts and words, we want to be the kinder person. Kindness keeps our energy or our vibration higher. Once protected, I asked Emma to communicate with the spirit through her mind. I asked her to acknowledge him, firmly tell him that she isn't comfortable with his presence and ask him to leave. If the spirit was wanting to work with her and she wasn't ready to do so, then she needed to tell him clearly that she wasn't ready. Always treat spirit with respect, nearly all spirit communications are made with love, they are not wanting to scare us. If you do not feel ready to open to spirit, like Emma, then that is your choice and they will understand. (It may not stop them trying again later, mind!)

Another tip I gave Emma was to 'pull in' her aura as it was wide open. You can do this simply by imagining the outside or edge of your energy field and visualise it shrinking inwards to next to your skin. Most mediums do the opposite when powering-up to connect with the spirit world; we do this under our own terms and give permission to spirit to step into our energy. Emma didn't feel ready to do this.

From my home, I connected into the gentleman and asked him to see the white light, to feel the energy of all his loved ones waiting for him and gently assured him it was time and safe for him to go into *the light. In my mind's eye, I saw him do this. I didn't hear back from Emma; the work had been completed. I just hope she keeps her 'light' down as she will attract other spirits, because being psychic, she is sending out unintentional signals.*

You may have heard of portals. These are energy centres that connect the physical and spiritual realms. You may have places, like in my aunt's house, where the energy changes. This could be temperature changes or a feeling of uncertainty. I remember as a child feeling like this at my aunt's. Her home was warm and inviting, yet as a young child, there was a spot in her hallway which felt cold as you walked through it. We (my cousins, sister and I) hated going upstairs on our own. We would bravely ascend the stairs to the toilet, then bolt downstairs in fear. The same too with my grandpa's house. My sister and I used to make a pact to go to the toilet together, wait for each other and then run down the stairs afterwards.

Portals can be both positive and negative, however, I believe that there isn't anything scary or evil in the spirit world, they are just gateways for spirit to pass through. Portals, or vortexes, have high natural energy when healing, helping spirit to pass over and ascension takes place. Healers and mediums can also be portals, their high vibration attracts spirits, but this will only happen if we leave ourselves open and are not careful to protect and close our energy down after we have finished working for the spirit world. Mediums are 'beacons of light', like a radar flashing into the spirit world giving them a clear signal that we are open, ready to connect and willing to work. Being open permanently can cause us to feel drained and exhausted which can lead to illness, so we need to make sure we are disciplined in our practice opening and closing.

There are several ways to cleanse a space from lower energies such as fear, anger, sadness, and these are by using the following methods. All methods are safe and easy to do, using intention and visualisation in some cases, however, if you feel that there is something darker or you have a portal, ask a respected medium to come in and to close the portal for you.

## Methods for Clearing a Space

- ° Crystals
- ° Smudging
- ° Visualisation
- ° Ask your Guardian Angel or the Archangels
- ° Call upon your loved ones
- ° Send healing, or if attuned, place the symbols around the room
- ° Say prayers
- ° Holy water

### Exercise to Open Up and Close Down

#### Opening Up

*Become aware of your breathing, breathe in deeply through your nose and slowly breathe out through your mouth. Breathe in... and out... in... and out...*

*Focus on your breath, in... and out... in... and out... Notice your heart rate becoming relaxed. In... and out... Relaxed.*

*Take your focus to the soles of your feet. Visualise roots growing out of them and growing into the Earth, Mother Earth. As your roots grow down, see them spreading wide, really anchoring you to the Earth and grounding you. When you are ready, on your next in-breath, draw up the Earth's energy up through the roots and send it round your body. Feel your muscles relaxing, your worries and tension disappearing and your whole body relaxing into the energy.*

*Now visualise a column or ball of shimmering white-golden light above your Crown chakra (head). This is the light of Spirit. Draw the white light down through your Crown to each chakra, the Crown, the Third Eye, the Throat, the Heart, the Solar Plexus, the Sacral, the Base chakra and finally through to the Earth Star under your feet. Now begin sending the white light of Spirit around your whole body. Breathe in the white light, filling your lungs. Fill your body with all the beautiful white light. Feel your body glowing with the white light, Spirit light. Feel yourself glowing with Spirit light. You are safe and protected.*

*Slowly expand your auric field. Expand it out in front of you as far as you can. Expand it behind you as far as you can, to the left, to the right, below your feet and above your head. You are surrounded by the white light of Spirit. You are safe and protected as you stand in the power of Spirit.*

*Feel the energy building, feel the energy becoming stronger. Your heart rate may increase as Spirit draws close. Ask your guides for a symbol to let you know when your energy is at full power.*

*Mentally ask your Guides, Loved Ones, Spirit Helpers and Ascended Masters to draw close and step into your energy. Bring them closer and closer. Feel their energy. Blend with their energy, becoming one. Feel their energy as it blends with yours.*

*Give thanks for their loving guidance and support.*

### Closing Down

*Visualise a ball of white light above your Crown chakra. Slowly bring it down over your aura sensing and knowing that as the ball of light travels downwards, it is clearing and cleansing any lower energies that you may have attracted. See it flow into Mother Earth who will transmute any lower energy into positive energy.*

# Chapter 23

# What Happens When We Die?

My development has guided me through many doors, and each path I take I feel I grow and develop a little more. Spiritual ascension happens when a person progresses spiritually and begins to evolve. This could be in the way they think, or how they understand themselves and the world around them. Instead of thinking solely about yourself, being led by the head, 'ego', you become more heart centred. As a person grows spiritually, they may begin to question life's bigger picture, understanding that we are all One and that we all have a role to play. The world isn't just about what you can get or what you have. Through ascension, you may explore these truths, find out how we are all connected and how to be of service in the world. Ascension is about returning home, being closer to The Divine, and individuals will notice a shifting of their energy, raising their vibration, clearing out the old, negative patterns which no longer serve them, and them leading a healthier, more meaningful life. A spiritual ascension can be a natural shift or can be the result of a life-changing experience. Although I have always been sensitive to the bigger picture, asking many questions about what happens when you die from an early age, becoming vegetarian at the age of 15 when nobody around me was (it just felt totally right not to eat a living creature) and being empathic within my job, teaching children with special needs, I realise now that I completely shifted when I had my first son. It took that shift to really open me up to the spirit world.

I believe, however, we continue to ascend, and ascension isn't complete until we cross over. There is so much to learn and experience, but everything happens as it should, and everyone will ascend at their own speed. We are individual souls with our own blueprint and our ascension will be exactly right for us, and the knowledge and understanding will come at the perfect time. The phrase, "When the student is ready, a teacher will appear", is exactly how it has been for me and the teacher isn't always a person. Books, movies, life experiences, overheard conversations, nature and the animal kingdom, they can all teach us. We simply need to listen!

Part Three

# The Mindfulness Approach

# Chapter 24

# Calmer Kids

Throughout my spiritual development I was teaching children with speech, language and communication difficulties. I taught children with ASD, ADHD, children with global learning needs and children who had/were neglected or abused. The more sensitive to spirit I became, the more I wanted to help these children grow emotionally. No longer was teaching children to read, write and count good enough, I wanted to heal them from the inside, help them to understand their feelings, organise their thought patterns and teach them how to remain calm, reduce their anger and anxiety, and learn how to understand their triggers. I wanted to introduce all children to mindfulness and healing.

One April when my boys were younger, we rented a holiday bungalow in North Wales. I remember vividly one night when everyone was sleeping, I sat bolt upright and had an urge to write. Wales always makes me feel close to nature and I believe that I'm extra sensitive and open there, so it didn't surprise me that as I sat down at the table with a cup of tea, I began to plan a complete programme to introduce children to mindfulness and healing. It was at a time when mindfulness wasn't a buzz word, and in fact, I hadn't even used the word 'mindfulness' once, but referred to the concept as meditation and emotions. That night, in the peace and quiet, with my family sleeping, I designed a perfect outline of sessions which would help children to become calm, explore their feelings, deal with their emotions and behaviours using their senses. I even saw an image in my mind's eye of a dandelion plant in seed with some seeds being blown. I was so excited but totally bewildered as to what it all meant. I needed sleep and collapsed into bed, exhausted but happy.

In the morning, it was the first thing that came into my mind. I could still feel the energy pulsating through my body at the realisation I'd channelled a system to help the children of our future. Breathing in the fresh aroma of my morning herbal tea, feeling serene, came the loud cries coming from the boy's bedroom. Charging in to see who had been hurt, I was presented with the realisation that they had knocked off a canvas picture hanging on the wall whilst bouncing on the beds. Rolling my eyes, but glad no one had broken any bones, I picked up the picture to see to my amazement a picture of a blown dandelion. Confirmation!

At the time I was working in a Speech and Language Base in Hertfordshire which I absolutely loved; however, I was beginning to see a pattern in the children in my care, and apart from their educational needs, they displayed emotional and behavioural needs too. My teaching was becoming not just educational, but I desperately wanted to help them on a more emotional and holistic level too. Trying to implement this within the education sector was difficult. At that time, we would cover friendships, how to communicate, even how to look after our mental and emotional self, even how to change our mindset, but the topics were covered at a basic level and 'ticked off' once done. There was no in-depth understanding of how the body works, how we can maintain a healthy mind or having regular time to 'check in' with ourselves. (Mindfulness has obviously improved within schools as I write this now, but it still isn't good enough in my opinion.)

One in ten children suffer from mental health problems, however, studies show that if children's mental health issues are addressed in childhood, then they are less likely to reoccur in adulthood. Problems such as depression, self-harm, generalised anxiety disorder (GAD), post-traumatic stress disorder and eating disorders are amongst the issues our children are facing today. I feel we also need to address the stresses we place upon our children, expecting better marks, peer pressure, increased responsibility, too much choice and involvement in adult affairs, social media and the Internet. These are making our children grow up faster than they need to, faster than they are possibly ready to. It is a more controlled and demanding world, unfortunately. Children are more aware of the pressures surrounding them, and many witness and hear things they shouldn't. They are wanting to, and are expected to, grow up too quickly and all this has massive implications on the way they deal with their emotions. I think some of this is relevant to us adults too. The need to be thin, clever, the best at something, be prettier/better looking, the list goes on and on. All of this results in feelings of stress, worry, anxiety and low self-esteem.

Children are usually unable to detect their stress and anxieties; it is often the symptoms which manifest that give us a clue to what is happening. Identifying stress and anxiety is only the tip of the iceberg, dealing with it can be complex for different reasons, but managing it is the way forward. Helping children to deal with such sensitive emotions can change their lives and allow them to be calm and focused, in control, and simply allow them to 'breathe'. So, my Calmer Kids programme was put into action. I designed it to help children pause and consider who they are and how they feel in a safe environment. Children often don't get the opportunity to self-reflect; they respond to issues quickly without thinking and often react, rather than dealing with their emotions first. Over time, this leads to behavioural problems.

With my carefully designed programme, it offered children the chance to breathe, take time out and build a relationship with themselves, bringing back self-choice and ultimately begin to understand themselves better. The sessions are conducted in a safe environment where the children will explore their senses through a range of exercises, help still their minds through relaxation techniques and meditation, and can 'talk' should they wish.

The programme also teaches them strategies in coping with issues and helping move them to living without fear. Using affirmations, the children can choose an area they would like to strengthen over the week in a positive way. The goal is for children to be able to apply learnt strategies for coping with stressful situations, to learn about themselves, begin to live their life and become confident.

Having worked with many children, I began to see a change. The parents began asking me if I taught this for adults, and families often wanted the sibling of the child I was working with to start too. From this evolved family sessions and I now teach an adult meditation class which I love. I feel blessed to be a medium, a teacher and work with children with my Calmer Kids program. I feel that I am being my 'true self' and am following my divine soul path.

# Chapter 25

# Meditation

*There are many different meditation techniques, some will still and soothe the mind, others take you on a journey into your soul.*

Meditation is a beautiful way to relax, however, what works well for one person will not always work for another. Some people will find meditation to still the mind and concentrate for longer periods harder than others, and many prefer the more complex adventures.

Being still or moving in quietness heightens our senses; in this state, you may begin to feel your body with sharper awareness. Our breath helps us to remain focused; using the breath can help us shift our awareness from the mind to the body, particularly the heart. Breathing rhythmically helps to increase the oxygen to the brain through our cells, giving us a surge of relaxed energy. Most of us are not breathing properly; it is shallow and often rapid, and in doing this, we are suppressing our emotions. Holding our breath or not breathing deeply locks our emotions and sends it deep within our soul, creating layer upon layer of built-up emotions and tension. Holding our breath tells the brain to fight or flight, sending a rush of adrenaline around our body. All this adrenaline builds up, and hence, over time we can become stressed. We all know that too much stress encourages our bodies to shut down, stop working in harmony and then, in turn, we become ill or depressed.

Bodies under stress, anxiety or upset, produce a chemical called cortisol. Our central nervous system is designed to instantly tell our adrenal glands to release adrenaline. Adrenaline is brilliant short term to create a reaction, however, over a period, it begins to have an adverse effect on our body. If we are subjected to stress over longer periods of time, we can suffer upset tummies, feel tension held in our muscles due to being unable to relax and hence this can intensify and become painful.

Meditation, a process of being able to shift consciousness, requires a person to reflect within and 'listen' or 'observe' what is happening in their own body. It is therefore a blissful and useful practice which will help you to study yourself, observe and assist you in understanding your emotions. In short, it is a beautiful gift to help you see the beauty of your inner world, your essence and enable you to develop a deeper appreciation of your emotions and who you are.

Although it is not connected to any religion, most religions practise meditation in some way.

Meditation seems easy, but it isn't as you will find that your mind wanders, thoughts pop in and you may get fidgety. Patience and practice is the key. Meditation may take time to perfect, it will not become natural overnight, but persist, continue and persevere or maybe make it a part of your daily routine because in time you will learn to depend upon it. It will be your friend, your teacher, your guide.

## Benefits of Meditation

- ☐ Helps to maintain calmness, less bothered by little things
- ☐ Balances energy resulting in better health
- ☐ Helps to train thoughts
- ☐ Improves mood and memory
- ☐ Inner peace
- ☐ Improves sleep
- ☐ Builds self-esteem
- ☐ Relaxes the body, mind and emotions
- ☐ Improves concentration and focus
- ☐ Decreases blood pressure

## How We Are Affected by Stress

- Sleeping too much or too little
- Becoming aggressive or hostile
- Irritability, moodiness
- Withdrawal from activities you used to like
- Crying
- Feeling fearful, anxious
- Suffering from headaches, tummy aches (physical symptoms)
- Becoming negative about themselves
- Repetitive tapping, cleaning of hands, or other OCD traits

Meditation is key to recognising emotions. It helps us to identify them, understand them, and as a result, we can address the difficulties, learn the triggers and become calmer and more relaxed.

## What Happens to Our Bodies When We Are Stressed?

- Breathing becomes faster as the lungs take in more oxygen.
- Systems which are involved in fighting infections are less likely to work effectively.
- Sweating may occur to cool us down.
- Pupils get larger to let in more light.
- The stress hormone, adrenaline, is secreted to keep this stress reaction going.
- The liver releases some of its store of glucose to fuel the muscles, ready to respond.
- The heart pumps harder to get the blood to where it is most needed in preparation for greater muscular effort. You may feel palpitations.
- There is therefore less blood elsewhere, skin may go pale and the movements to the stomach slow down or stop. (Sinking feeling.)
- The intestines become less active and salivary glands dry up.

Relaxation is the best way to help us cope with stress, however, it can be very hard for us to do this, so try to introduce relaxation into your day. Doing fun things which you enjoy will shift your moods and help you create positivity. Taking time for yourself is important too, a long bath, a walk in the countryside or park, spending time with the family or petting an animal. Playing sports, yoga, reading a good book, meeting up with friends and of course meditation are all ways to wind down. In this relaxed state, you will feel closer to spirit and will be able to hear, sense, see their signs which they are sending you. It is also a wonderful way for you to remove the worries and stresses that are constantly circling your mind. As your mind quietens, you will become aware of your body and focusing on the different body parts can be an extremely effective way to listen to your thoughts and feelings and understand your body's needs. The body whispers to us, by being calm we can listen. When the body shouts, it's often a wake-up call; we don't need those wake-up calls, listen to the whispers. It's the whispers that guide us.

Breathing – slow, deep, long breaths in and out help to increase the oxygen intake into our bodies and particularly our brains. Try it, it really works!

## The Present

We are here, living exactly as we are meant to. Everything is how it is supposed to be in this present time. Although at times, it may seem that life is difficult or challenging. It is not because we have been bad, but it is because we are meant to be experiencing the very lesson for our soul's growth. Be patient whilst our teaching is being presented to us, see the opportunity of growth and learn to be grateful for the experience. As we grow, we expand and deepen our consciousness. Through this we begin to see and feel differently. Be open to opportunities which arise and take the hand of fate who knows what is good for us. See the joy or growth which is being presented and be excited as it takes us further along our path of enlightenment. Know you are guided and protected along your way; even the most difficult times can't last forever. Life is a journey, be kind to yourself, forgive along the way, and love, yourself and others. From the storm we see the rainbows of hope which give evidence that life continues. It is a journey, not a linear one but one that deepens our soul's path. Enjoy the process as it builds and enriches, give thanks for the lessons learnt.

Experience everything that is going on around you, the seasons of growth and maturity. Acknowledge the learning within and trust the process. Relax and look for the secrets as you accomplish your goals.

You are guided.

## The Gift of the Present Moment

Our world is a beautiful place, there is so much to discover and so much to experience.

We can only do this if we are living in the present moment. Worrying about the past is futile, a waste of energy as we can't change it and feeling anxious about the future is also using up unnecessary energy as the future never materialises. We have all heard the saying, "Tomorrow never comes." Usually, our worries and concerns rarely unfold as we imagine, and we certainly have no direct control over most situations, we can only control ourselves. In fact we can only control our reactions as our emotions naturally occur when we least expect them. Choosing to stay in the present moment means that we can appreciate what is happening all round us. Each flower, delicately emerging from a tight bud, the tiny insects which flutter their lacy wings, the bright sun rising each morning and the silvery moon glistening in the dark, starry sky. The sea lapping the golden sand, the trees gently swaying in the breeze or the calling of birds as they communicate with each other. All these amazing experiences we would miss if we allowed our worrying minds to take over and consume us.

Anxiety, worry, anger or sadness are all normal human emotions which everyone feels time after time at some point, but we can learn to switch them off too, silencing the thoughts that spin round and around. Spending time with ourselves, sitting quietly, out in nature, exercising or doing something which occupies the mind like colouring, cooking, painting, sewing, building or creating will keep us focused and hence keep our racing brains from running away and spiralling. In this light meditative state, we can simply BE. We can appreciate the HERE and NOW, the beauty and magic of LIFE.

Try this daily to stay in the present and connect with yourself:

### Breathing Technique

*Make sure you are sitting comfortably with your feet flat on the floor and your arms by your side. Close your eyes and take a big breath in through your nose, filling your lungs. Slowly breathe out of your mouth. Breathe in... and out. As you breathe in, know that you are breathing all the goodness from around you, and as you breathe out, breathe out any worries or troubles. Feel yourself becoming calm and relaxed as you breathe in and out. Let any thoughts float away, they are not important right now. Just keep breathing in and out, calm and relaxed.*

*As you breathe in deeply feel all the lovely, calm air circle around your feet. Notice how they feel. Are they hot, warm, cold? Let go and relax, feel them becoming floppy. Breathe and relax.*

*Breathe into your legs, relax all your muscles and sense how they feel. Beautiful. Breathe and relax.*

*Think about your tummy, notice how soft it is. Breathe deeply into your tummy and feel the air flowing around. Relax, breathe out through the nose.*

*Focus on your hands. Open your hands, palms facing upwards and let the feeling of any tension go. Breathe and relax your hands.*

*Take your attention to your shoulders. Raise them up towards your ears and let them flop. Breathe and relax.*

*Feel all the tension in your body melting. Floating away. Your body feels heavy as it lies on the floor. Breathe and relax.*

*Take a deep breath in through your nose... and slowly breathe out through your mouth.*

*Spend some moments being still.*

*Wiggle your fingers and toes, and when you are ready, open your eyes and simply observe all you can see, feel or hear around you and SMILE.*

## Conscious Breathing for Health Benefits

Think about your breathing, become aware of how your breaths enter and exit from your body. Notice how many times you breathe in and out during a minute. You probably haven't even considered your breathing before in detail unless you have been exercising and then you become aware of how shallow it is. Throughout the day, we take it for granted.

It is known amazingly that around 70% of our toxins are released from our body through our breath. Of these toxins, carbon dioxide is a natural waste product of our body's metabolism, so breathing deeply helps us to rid our body of it, allowing our systems to work more efficiently. In contrast, oxygen is the most essential natural resource needed by our cells, and the deeper we breathe, the more oxygen we receive.

Just think, we can go without food for up to 40 days, water for three days and yet we can die after just a few minutes of not breathing!

When we are not breathing correctly, and most of us are not, what we are doing is suppressing our emotions. We mask our feelings by drawing in our breath and holding it because our breathing is our protection; it's that short sharp intake when we are scared or shocked, when we are surprised. When you are anxious and your body is under stress, have you noticed how your breathing quickens? Anxiety, the fight or flight, instinctive response of a difficult situation.

Holding our breath and locking it away creates layer upon layer of built-up emotions. When we hold our breath, it triggers the brain and prepares it to fight or flight. When we are stressed, anxious or upset, our bodies produce a chemical called cortisol and our central nervous system instantly tells our adrenal glands to release adrenaline. This rush of adrenaline is pumped around our body, and as this adrenaline builds the more stressed we become. Too much stress encourages our bodies to shut down as high levels of adrenaline put pressure on our internal organs and they simply can't function effectively. Eventually we become ill or depressed.

Breathing deeply and rhythmically helps to increase the oxygen to the brain through our cells, giving us a surge of energy. Conscious breathing, as it is called, is a powerful way to flood our body with oxygen, recharging us at cellular levels, bringing healing, higher levels of consciousness, mental and emotional clarity and helping us to strengthen our connection with our self – understanding who we truly are.

**A little science:** The lungs are not muscles; they cannot move air without help. The muscles for the upper torso and neck only play a minor role and alone only allow us to breathe in small amounts of air – clavicular breathing (emphysema). The intercostal muscles that lie between the ribs account of around 20% of normal breathing, but again, can make breathing laboured. Breathing in this way arouses the sympathetic nervous system and maintains levels of tension that sap energy and increase emotional distress.

It is the diaphragm that is naturally used to expand the lungs during breathing. As we breathe in the diaphragm contracts pulling down, which expands the lungs, and at the same time the abdominal organs are compressed and press out against the abdominals. When we exhale, the diaphragm relaxes, causing the ribs to shrink.

Another aspect to consider is the Vagus nerve. This is a cranial nerve that runs from your brain through your neck and chest to your abdomen and is linked to the effectiveness of our moods, heart rate, digestion, and immune system, in fact all organs which are affected by anxiety and stress. The name 'Vagus nerve' comes from the Latin word for *wandering* which is perfect as it has many connections and branches through the body, just like a tree. Visualise a tree, with its grounding roots spread wide beneath the ground, anchoring us to the Earth. See the strong, protective trunk which is largely unbreakable in strength, bringing protection and the fine yet flexible and durable branches with their green leaves which absorb the air, sunlight and water for food. Then you can begin to see how the Vagus nerve, like a tree, is central and vital for balance and health; we can't ignore the link between stomach upsets, palpitations, mood changes and poor health when we are anxious for a period of time. So, it is important to know that research has shown it is possible to stimulate the Vagus nerve through breathing, helping our organs to function better.

### Breathing technique – a little exercise
*Light a candle to help you focus or close your eyes.*

*Become aware of your breathing, be aware of where you are and how your body feels and then begin to focus on every muscle, breathing into it and feeling it relax. Relax your feet, legs and pelvis. Relax your stomach, the chest, your spine and shoulders. Feel your neck and jaw relax and soften your eyes.*

*Now concentrate on breathing in through your nose and out of your mouth, repeat this several times as your body starts to respond to the natural rhythm of breathing.*

*Each time you breathe in, make it longer and deeper. (Don't force your intake, don't gasp or hold your breath.)*

*Every exhale is slower and softer. (Don't force it out.)*

*See your breath like a circular motion, flowing in, wafting around your body, then releasing, being removed through your mouth.*

*Visualising a colour may help you trace the flow of your breath.*

*And just keep breathing, every time your focus shifts, bring it back to the breath, becoming aware of the rise and fall of your ribcage.*

*Slow, steady, rhythmical breathing. In and out, inhaling and exhaling.*

*(Continue for as long as you feel it takes to bring your body into a state of calm and balance. At least ten minutes if you can.)*

*How amazing do you feel? Did you experience the rush of oxygen racing to your head, light-headedness maybe? Is your breathing slower? What about your heartbeat, is it slower too? You should be feeling calmer and relaxed, less anxious or stressed, and be marvelling in better mental and emotional clarity.*

# Chapter 26

# Colour Healing

Colour is everywhere, all around us. Colour determines our skin tone, our eyes and hair. It dominates the clothes we wear, the objects we have in our home, and we even choose items depending on our favourite colour.

More astonishing is colour is abundant in nature. Within the plant kingdom and in the animal kingdom, colour is all about survival, it is a hidden language. Animals use camouflage to protect themselves, they send out secret messages to attract a partner or herald a warning.

We absorb colour energy through our eyes and skin, or we can ingest it through liquid and food. When we see colour, our brain and nervous systems are stimulated which can have an effect on our energy, working on a deeper level of our physical, mental, emotional and spiritual being.

Although light appears colourless, it holds all the colours and each colour has its own vibration or 'wavelength', carrying its unique healing energy. We have a natural sensitivity to colour, and even if you are blind, you may be able to 'feel' or 'sense' colour.

Colour has also been important in all religions and carries symbology. In Christianity, we wear white at weddings to symbolise purity or virginity, purple is seen as spiritual or royal, and Buddhist monks wear orange to represent humility. In the Hindu religion, yellow represents life and truth, whereas Ancient Rome associated red with Mars and war. Black has long been identified with superstition and death.

On that note, I am a person who usually wears black. I've always worn black, but I do love colour. For me, colour is an amazing tool for healing. I will pick a coloured scarf or jewellery to brighten up my clothes and I have usually chosen that colour because I need its energy.

Like crystals, colour carries an energy, a vibration which can affect our mood. There are many lists out there, but being intuitive, I like to feel the energy and encourage you to do the same. I will give you my interpretation, but again like I have said throughout this book, meaning must make sense to you and not be acquired from someone else. It is how you feel.

Our aura, the energy around us, is filled with colour which can say a great deal about how we are feeling and help us to identify illness. The first layer of our aura, the etheric body, is like a sieve allowing energy to flow into and out of our physical body. It is like a gateway. The second layer is called the astral layer, sometimes also called the emotional body, and the colours seen here reflect our mood and emotions. The third layer is called the mental body, and like it suggests, projects our thoughts. Our aura, in some respect, is our protection and if we can keep our thoughts positive, then what flows into our body is positive. On the other hand, if our thoughts are dark, anxious or worried then we allow that energy to flow through, and once it filters through the astral layer, it will enter our body and thus have a direct influence on our organs causing disharmony and potentially making us ill. This is because the negative vibrations change the energy of our body, making us ill.

Keeping our body tip-top in good vibrational energy is therefore hugely important to our health. By altering your thought patterns, ingesting certain colours and placing specific colours which inspire, excite, calm or relax you, then you can move through life in a positive way and direct the right healing vibration into your auric field.

A lovely meditation I do myself and with others is to visualise a bubble around yourself and fill it with a colour. It is important to allow your Higher Self to give you the colour as it will be the colour you need. It should be the first colour that springs into your mind and not your favourite colour. Don't worry if you don't like the colour, sometimes we need things we do not realise we need. This exercise is not only healing, but it will help you to understand your emotions at the time of the meditation. For example, if you choose blue, it could be because you are stressed and need calm. If you choose orange, you may be lacking creativity, green for healing and yellow for inspiration. Red can represent love to some, or anger, like a red rag to a bull, however, if they choose to put it in their bubble then they are probably needing energy.

Try bringing colour into your life and notice how it begins to change your moods and emotions for the better. Choosing crystals is based on the same principle: we feel drawn to a crystal for its properties but also for its colour.

## Understanding Colour

| Colour | Energy |
|--------|--------|
| Red | Warming, energising, stimulating, grounding, brings strength, courage and perseverance |
| Orange | Stimulates the digestive system, low immunity, exhaustion, joy and happiness |
| Yellow | Wisdom, inspiration, happiness, sunny |
| Green | Love, beauty, environment, healing |
| Blue | Peace, calm, communication, tranquil, thoughtful, quietness |
| Purple | Spiritual, imagination, dreams, intuition, healing, protection |
| Pink | Calm, happy, love family, kindness, gentleness |

| Black | Protection |
|-------|------------|
| White | Protection, cleansing, purity, stillness, quietness |

Below is a beautiful meditation. As you go through the journey in your mind, you come to a beach and are invited to enter the ocean. As the water washes over you it changes colour bringing healing.

## The Healing Ocean

*Close your eyes.*
*See/visualise yourself on a glorious beach with the clear blue sky, the warmth of the sun and a vast ocean in front of you. Notice how the sun glistens on the water, sparkling, shimmering, and as you take a deep breath in, begin to feel a calmness washing over you. Every breath in, you feel more and more relaxed.*
*Feel your feet standing or sinking into the soft golden sand. Feel the softness of the sand beneath your feet and take a moment to relax deeper, then send any tension held within your body down through the soles of your feet into the sand.*
*The vast blue-green ocean is inviting you to enter, so slowly you wade into it; first your toes wiggle in the warm water, then both your feet. Before you know it, you have ventured further and further into the water, up to your tummy, and you notice that the water is sparkling. You feel happy and safe here, and slowly lower your body down until the water surrounds you, like in a warm bath.*
*Small bubbles begin to rise out of the ocean, all different colours – red, purple, blue, green, yellow, orange, silver, gold, turquoise.*
*Watch them rise and pop, rise and pop, rise and pop. Every time this happens, you realise that any of your worries or troubles seem to disappear and soon you have no worrying or angry thoughts, you are calm and relaxed and happy.*

*As the warm sparkling water washes over your skin and muscles it relaxes them. Feel your toes, feet and ankles relax, your legs and tummy relax. Feel your spine and shoulders relax, your arms, hands and fingers relax. Notice your neck and face relax. Your whole body relaxed, being supported by the water.*

*Now your body has relaxed, the healing begins. The sparkling, bubbling water heals all aspects of your body, in and out. As you breathe in, the healing travels around your body, as you breathe out, you breathe out all the emotions, pains, worries you no longer wish to carry inside of you. You release feelings of regret, guilt, sadness, anxiety. With your next breath in, you breathe in hopefulness, courage, confidence and acceptance. Feel your body swelling with goodness and notice how wonderful you feel.*

*Finally, you dip your head under the water for one last healing cleanse, and as you emerge, you notice how much better you feel. Positive, smiling and full of love.*

*Music*

*Know that the ocean is cleansing your energy, clearing and allowing your emotions to flow. Draw strength from this and let your troubles go, trust, trust that when you are able to go with the flow, your life will move forwards, open up in the right way for you. Let go of control. Breathe in and out.*

*Music*

*Bringing yourself back to your own awareness by taking a beautiful deep breath in and out. Wiggle your fingers and toes, and when you are ready, open your eyes.*

# Chapter 27

# Aligning Our Mind, Emotions and Behaviours

Parents can pass down trauma from their own upbringing, linked to genes. I believe this is true about past lives too.

*How we parent has an important impact on our children's mental health.*

When our bodies are stressed, it produces adrenaline which is a hormone produced in the medulla in the adrenal glands. It is often referred to as the 'fight or flight' hormone that helps us to prepare for danger. Adrenaline is quickly released into the blood and to the specific organ to begin a response. It helps to open the passageways for increased oxygen which is then delivered to the muscles, including the heart and lungs, making them react, even if in pain because adrenaline decreases our ability to feel pain. Adrenaline also has an impact on our strength and performance, lasting over an hour from when it has been released.

Although this seems a positive thing, it has its downside. Too much adrenaline can result in feeling faint or light-headed, and when we are constantly under stress, we can become tired, irritable, anxious and depressed. If we do not need the excess chemicals or oxygen then our bodies act against us, the decreased $CO_2$ levels in the lungs and the blood supply make us disorientated, hyperventilate or have a panic attack.

## Oxytocin – 'Positive Touch' Hormone
Oxytocin is produced in the hypothalamus and secreted by the pituitary gland. It has an anti-anxiety effect which reduces stress responses. Oxytocin is released when breastfeeding.

Low levels of oxytocin have been linked to depression.

**Daily Tips:**
- Meditation
- Exercise
- Breathing techniques
- Identify your worries but don't give in to their power
- Use positive affirmations
- Look at pictures of a relaxing place, use your senses to connect in with a calming environment

Don't try to stop your thoughts, they are a natural process. However, learn to live with them by turning them into a positive action.

## Young Children and Teens

Much debate surrounds this topic, especially as it gets the children to engage with their emotions, however, I feel that we can underestimate their ability to understand themselves, and through modelling and game-based techniques, children should be able to respond to the programme.

**Ways to engage children:**
- Puppets
- Stories – guided or open
- Games
- Problem solving
- Pictures, visual prompts
- Visualisations
- Non-verbal ways – thinking bubbles, diagrams, cartoon clips, rating scales, charts

There is good evidence that supporting children and teens with emotional and behavioural issues should be approached in a

3-step way. Firstly, develop a clear understanding of the child's problems, how they are affecting them and what behaviours are displayed. Next develop and promote specific skills and strategies to help the child cope with his/her problems in an encouraging way which makes them feel safe and is manageable for them to achieve. Lastly, set interventions to help with identifying, testing and reappraising general dysfunctional cognitions and behaviours. This is important to help to prepare the child for a potential relapse.

This process helps children, teens or adults who are suffering with anxiety disorders, depression, obsessional compulsive disorder and post-traumatic stress disorder.

The basics of the above method are used by cognitive behavioural therapists and this therapy focuses on the relationship between the following:

- Cognitions – what we think
- Affect – how we feel
- Behaviour – what we do

Studies have shown that:

- Emotional responses can become conditioned to specific events (Wolpe, 1958).
- Emotional responses can be reciprocally inhibited (Skinner, 1974) – a certain behaviour increases in frequency because it has been followed by a positive (or not negative) consequence.
- Learning could occur by watching someone else, and it proposed a model of self-control based on self-observation, self-evaluation and self-reinforcement (Banura, 1977).
- Behaviour under the control of thoughts or internal speech. Changing self-instructions can lead to the development

of more appropriate self-control techniques. A 4-stage process of observing someone doing a task, being talked through the same task by another person, talking oneself through the task aloud and whispering instructions (Meichenbaum, 1975).

- Behaviour is influenced by cognitive events and processes.
- Changing cognitive processes can lead to changes in behaviour.
- Young (1990) proposed that maladaptive cognitive schemas that are formed in childhood lead to self-defeating patterns of behaviour which are repeated throughout life. The maladaptive schemas are associated with certain parenting styles, and they develop if the basic emotional needs of the child are not met.

CBT is about understanding how events and experiences are interpreted. It supports us in understanding and changing the distortions we think and feel that occur in cognitive processing.

Aaron Beck's work/model is based on how early parenting and experiences lead to the development of fixed ways of thinking. New information and experiences are assessed against these core beliefs e.g., "I must be successful", and information that reinforces and maintains them is selected and filtered. Core beliefs are triggered by or activated by important events e.g., taking exams, and these lead to a few assumptions e.g., "I will only be successful and pass if I study all day." These give rise to automatic thoughts e.g., "I must be stupid," or "I will never pass." These automatic thoughts lead to emotional changes e.g., stress, anxiety and can lead to the person staying in, not sleeping, overeating etc.

### The Cognitive Model*

*Core belief formed during childhood*
*Important events activate core beliefs*

*Core beliefs trigger cognitive assumptions*
*Assumptions produce automatic thoughts*
*Automatic thoughts generate responses*
*Emotional responses. Behavioural responses. Somatic responses.*
*Based on Aaron Beck's work – Beck Institute Model

# Chapter 28

# Affirmations

Have you ever told yourself, over and over again, that you are useless at something? It may be a subject, like maths or spelling, it could be cooking, painting or even singing. I know I have in the past and I've said it for so long that I truly believed it, I even laughed about it and told other people. It is what I considered to be true.

Have you ever told yourself how good you are at something? Probably not, that would be boasting, singing your own praises. In fact, when somebody compliments you, you play it down. You don't always believe them or can think of many other people who can do it better.

But why? Why do we do this to ourselves? It programmes our subconscious mind to believe it. Negativity said so many times becomes a truth. In fact, negative thoughts can affect our mood, confidence and self-esteem. Constantly thinking negative thoughts can make our general outlook negative and we can become depressed.

What if we only told ourselves positive things? I am good at maths, I am a wonderful cook, I am happy, I am healthy, I am capable of producing great work, I'm calm and relaxed, I am a successful businessperson, I am loved, I am a caring, supportive friend, etc. Positive statements affirmed repeatedly are picked up by our subconscious mind. The mind, upon receiving them, will in turn believe them to be true. We become these things in our mind and our energy reflects it.

Positive affirmations send positive thoughts about who we are to the brain, which in turn releases chemicals related to that emotion. In short, the effectiveness of positive affirmations lies within linking them to our emotions. Experiencing how good we feel when we say affirmations is powerful, it can be a tricky way of thinking, but positive affirmations work and have been used successfully to treat people with low self-esteem. It can be wonderful for those 'glass is half empty' types.

Repeating positive statements daily, with the added use of visualisation and goal setting, will encourage and support us in turning negative comments about ourselves around, changing the way we think about who we are. Believe me, you really can retrain your brain to be more positive, to believe in yourself, and in turn, boost your confidence.

Whilst I acknowledge some people's views of 'lying to yourself' and 'temporarily making ourselves feel better' or 'it is an escape from looking at the truth', I believe that we need to look at the whole picture, understand our emotions and deal with them. It is not about brushing our fears and worries aside, but listening to them, acknowledging them, dealing with them and healing them. Positive affirmations can help us to do exactly that.

Examples:
"I am perfect just as I am."
"I lovingly respect myself."
"I am happy, I'm healthy, I'm safe."

*Maybe you can think of some of your own!*

# Chapter 29

# Opening the Heart Chakra

*With my loving embrace I offer you compassion and support for your journey in this lifetime. Surrender your heart to me so I can hold you, guide you and love you.*
*– Archangel Mary (channelled by Alison Grey)*

The Heart chakra is located within our chest, it is our fourth chakra or our sixth chakra if you are on your Ascension path. The fourth chakra is green, and our sixth chakra is pink, and it looks like a flower with 33 petals. As you might remember, 33 is the vibration of Jesus Christ and our Heart chakra carries his magnificent energy. Archangel Chamuel oversees our Heart chakra; he is the angel of love. When we open our Heart chakra we are opening to love, to giving and receiving love, including self-love.

So many people rush around day in and day out, there is the importance of achieving and racing to the top. Money needs to be made and we can be judged by the holidays we take, the size of our houses, the cars in our drives and the possessions we have. We are deemed 'successful' or 'powerful' if we have well-paid jobs and a huge salary. However, the phrase, "You can't take it with you when you die," is so true, and in the Spirit World, we are not congratulated by our wealth but by being true, kind, helpful, loving.

Our brains and bank balances do not travel with us when we pass over, and our body is left behind as only the soul goes home. It doesn't matter to spirit if you are tall, short, large or petite. They are not concerned about how toned your body is, your hair or how pretty you are. The only thing which matters is your heart and soul. Yes, we need to keep healthy, our body is our home while on this Earth, so we need to take good care of it, but all the above is what we, with earthly minds, feel is important. In truth, it is our heart and how we have treated others, the good deeds we have accomplished and how we have loved that is important. Think back to the Ancient Egyptians, Anubis weighing the heart against a feather. This image is exactly how I see it too. Our body is a vessel, a mighty great one but just a home for our spirit while wars are visiting in this incarnation.

To successfully open the Heart chakra, we need to move our energy from the mind (the ego) to the heart where we can bridge the gap between the human and the soul. Our minds motivate us, they give us the push we need to get things done, help us to be organised, proactive and successful; the heart is intuitive. The heart feels, cares, loves, embraces, forgives and can be hurt easily. When blocked, we can feel negative, unworthy, insecure, let-down or lost. Caught up in these emotions, we begin to judge ourselves.

An open heart understands, it can see through the pain and understands the bigger picture. It can start the process of self-acceptance, self-love and self-forgiveness and forgiveness of others.

One way to open our Heart chakra is through empathy, understanding how others feel, expressing our truth and loving. Loving others, our parents, our children, our pets and friends, opens our hearts and radiates love, but first we must begin to love ourselves because to find happiness you must first look within.

Spend a few moments to consider what your life's purpose is. What is it that you desire? Deep question – yes, but a question that many people ask of themselves and a question that worries more people than you realise. To not know who you are, where you fit in or how you make a difference in the world is natural as we all want to feel connected, grounded and loved.

One way to explore these questions is to go within, listen to our hearts and notice what makes us elated, smile, increases our energy levels or causes excitement. What do you daydream about? What aspects of your relationships bring enormous joy? Look at your hobbies, an indication of how you enjoy spending your free time is a vital clue, and see if there is a pattern or a common theme.

Children have wonderful, creative dreams about what they want to be when they grow up, however, some people agonise over this and many still don't know as they enter adulthood. But this isn't really about what you want to be, the purpose of this is to understand yourself. To feel happy in your own skin, and to accept and be happy with who you are. Devoting time to the things which bring us pleasure will allow our hearts to sing and our minds to calm. You will feel elated by the time and energy you invest in yourself.

Joy reminds us that we are not suffering, and finding out who we are and what makes us happy brings us joy, healing and a sense of connectedness. We can heal through the power of joy. By letting go of our fears or restrictive thinking we are opening ourselves up to the miracles of healing and helping us find joy inside.

So spend some time investing in yourself, be creative, meditate, enjoy a walking meditation – merging your energy within nature's energy, absorbing their gifts they offer us readily, have a healing session or enjoy hobbies that expand the creative brain that stimulates the production of endorphins. Surround yourself with positive colours, scents, images, crystals and upbeat people who won't drain your energy or pollute it. Connect with yourself, be true to yourself and know that whatever you do, you will make a difference to somebody, bring love to someone and be loved by a very special person/ people. Be kind to yourself by rehearsing positive statements about yourself and control the negative thoughts of anxiety, guilt, worries and low confidence which affect your energy. If we are true to ourselves then we can't go wrong. This is the healing power of joy and an open-heart centre, as is practising compassion towards others.

Occasionally an awakening may need to occur to jolt us back onto the right path, our soul's path. An initiation may be presented to us to help make us feel like something is missing, there must be a higher purpose, or that we simply can't keep making the wrong choices and repeating the same negative patterns. This initiation will be gifted to us (however difficult that may sound), so we can work on our heart centre and begin living with an open heart.

### Guided Meditation for the Heart Chakra
### Archangel Chamuel

*Sitting comfortably, close your eyes and become aware of your breath. Breathe in deeply through your nose, filling your lungs, and then slowly breathe out. Breathe in all that is good for you, and as you exhale, release any tensions and worries. Breathing in... and out... in... and out. Feel your body becoming more and more relaxed.*

*Visualise a ball of protective light surrounding you. You are safe and protected as you breathe in and out.*

*Focusing on your breathing, visualise yourself breathing in through your nose, and as you exhale, exhale through your Heart chakra. Breathing in through the nose, exhale out of the Heart. Keep repeating this, breathing into your nose and out of your through your Heart.*

*Call upon Archangel Chamuel, the angel of love in his pink and white ray, who helps us with all aspects of the heart.*

*Focus your attention on your Heart chakra. See Archangel Chamuel placing his angelic, healing hands over your heart, sending a beautiful soft pink healing light into your heart centre.*

*Inhale deeply, drawing in the pink light and feel it healing your physical and your emotional heart.*

*Set the intention for Archangel Chamuel to help you release any pain or traumatic experiences which you have been holding on to. Ask him to help you to let go of any energy which no longer serves you. Ask him to bring about self-forgiveness and forgiveness to others who have hurt you.*

*Breathe in the pink light, and as you slowly exhale, release anything that has been weighing your heart down. As you exhale this old energy, Archangel Chamuel too will transmute the pain energy into high vibrational energy and positive energy.*

*Breathe in deeply again and notice how your heart is feeling lighter, clearer, even sparkling. Ask your heart if it has a message for you. These may appear to you as thoughts, feelings, note any temperature changes or tingles and know that you are receiving angelic guidance.*

*Ask your Heart chakra, either silently or aloud: What changes you would like to see me make in my life so that I can open even more? Again, acknowledge any thoughts, visions, colours etc.*

*Affirm to yourself that you are loved. Affirm you are in the right place for where you need to be. Know you are strong and protected. Trust and believe this.*

*Notice how your Heart chakra begins to expand, see the 33 pink and white petals grow brighter and clearer. Allow this gift of love to resonate into your very being and then send it to others who may also need this beautiful heart healing energy.*

*Take a deep breath in... and as you exhale, bring your awareness back into the room. Wiggle your fingers and toes, and when you are ready, open your eyes.*

## Affirmations, Quotes and Positive Statements

Like affirmations, quotes and words of hope produce some powerful statements which we tell and remind ourselves. Looking at these uplifting sentences help to trigger our subconscious mind to allow ourselves to believe. They give us permission to accept and understand a truth, and with this, we can be what we believe. Positive gratitude statements and words of hope bring a smile to our faces, a warmth and inner-hugs to us which open our hearts and open us up to the possibility of change – for our highest good.

Below are a few of my favourite gratitude and positivity statements and positive quotes from my Calmer Kids Facebook page.

"Happiness does not depend on what happens outside of you, but on what happens inside of you." (QuotesBlog.net)

"Today I will not stress over things I can't control."

"If you want your life to be a magnificent story, then begin by realising you are the author." (Mark Houlahan)

"You can't use up creativity. The more you use, the more you have." (Maya Angelou)

"Being kind to yourself is one of the greatest kindnesses," said the Mole. (*The Boy, the Mole, the Fox and the Horse* by Charlie Mackesy)

"Count your rainbows, not your thunderstorms." (Alyssa Knight, aged 12)

"I radiate gratitude for the calm and peace in my life."

"I radiate happiness and trust all is well."

"I am grateful for the love in my life and feel blessed to have a supporting family beside me."

"I am thankful for my Spiritual gifts, so that I can work for the Divine to help others."

There are so many more. Each time I read a quote or statement, I can feel myself becoming lighter and moving closer to my soul as the words resonate.

# Chapter 30

# Prayers

Prayers are often thought of as pleas, desperate begs of something better that you send to God via the angels. How often have you brought your hands together and begun to say, "Please God..."? Maybe you have bargained with Him to help you in your hour of need and in return will sacrifice something or be prepared to do something – "... And I promise I will ..." I know I have.

Have you ever noticed that even though you beg for an outcome, help hasn't always come? You didn't get that job you wanted, you didn't win the money on the lottery, even though if you had you would give a chunk to charity, and the cycle of events which you hoped would stop, kept occurring. Have you noticed that some prayers come to fruition whilst others don't? I can also hear people asking, well I thought if I asked for the angels' assistance, then they can intervene – so why don't they?

Consider this thought, prayers will only work if they are for your highest and greatest good and the highest and greatest good of others if you are praying for something involving another person or persons. Prayers are carried by angels to the Divine, to God as they are winged messengers; they will also bring us the answers in forms of signs and gentle nudging. But, if it isn't in line with your soul's purpose, if it will have a negative impact on another person or it isn't part of the 'plan' as it's a lesson you need to learn, then you may not receive your wishes. This doesn't mean that the angels let you get on with it and dismiss your prayers; they will comfort you, guide you and help you understand the lesson to be learnt.

Another important aspect to understand with prayers is that I believe they work when you affirm your gratitude of them already happening. Kyle Gray (*The Angel Whisperer*) introduced this concept, and as I looked back over my gratitude practice which I have been doing for years, I could see the pattern. Thanking the angels for already delivering your prayers for the highest and greatest good is the same as blessing a crystal, laying out a crystal grid and making a vision board: it is all about 'intention' and the messages you are sending to yourself and the Universe. It is the gratitude of saying, "Thank you for supporting/guiding me towards..." as if it has already happened, already been manifested.

I truly believe too in the power of 'collective prayers' and have seen and experienced the results of healing, through collective prayers given to a person whose recovery was prayed for. Any prayer will be powerful if asked for the highest and greatest good, is in line with your soul's purpose, asked with gratitude and thanks. Manners go a long way!

Below are some examples.

"Thank you for helping me see the beauty all around, reminding me that nature soothes and relaxes me."

"Thank you for reminding me how to feel joy in my heart, for smiling through the difficult times, keeping faith in my heart."

We are all made of energy, everything is energy and we are in control of how we use our energy. To communicate we give off energy which people and animals can read, so it is important we use our energy kindly, that way we can change the energy that we receive back. The exchange of energy can mean the difference between happiness and sadness, between laughter and anger. Try sending out positive energy and see how it feels to receive some back.

Acts of kindness and being kind to yourself create a multitude of positive benefits. Think about the ripple effect of a smile: when somebody smiles at you, immediately you smile back. The warmth of the smile spreads throughout your body and raises your spirits. It brings many truths; you are noticed, appreciated, thanked, you realise that the human race is indeed lovely and that happiness can come at the divine time to cheer you up or help you forget your worries – just for a moment. It brings reality and hope too. Do you know that spreading happiness, this could be in many ways, stimulates the production of serotonin, our feel-good hormone helping us feel calm and relaxed? It also reduces the cortisol levels in our bodies, lowering the risks of our inner organs such as the heart. Cortisol is responsible for the increase in our stress and anxiety levels. Being happy releases oxytocin within our bodies helping us to feel safe, loved and bonded, just like a huge hug.

Consider kindness, to yourself and others, as a karmic gift. The gift of love, the gift of appreciation, the gift of the present moment, the gift of deep listening, and with all these gifts comes the realisation that being kind has a positive effect on your mind, body and soul. Try it and see those ripples as they spread far and wide.

# Chapter 31

# Herbs for Health and Essential Oils

I am not a practising herbologist, even though I often dream of becoming one, but herbs and plants fascinate me, and I totally believe in their natural ability to treat or cure. These are gifts of nature that can aid, soothe or cure almost any ailment or emotion. Herbal medicine is a holistic practice which dates as far back as the Neanderthal period, and herbs are not just used for cooking. In fact, even most pharmaceuticals are derivatives from plants.

Using herbs and plants help to naturally bring the body into balance, and it is often said that the Earth has everything we need to heal our bodies and I believe this to be true. Take the animal kingdom for example, it intuitively knows what to eat to heal itself.

**Ways we can use herbs and plants:**
- Swallowed as pills, powders, or tinctures
- Brewed as tea
- Applied to the skin as gels, lotions, or creams
- Added to bath water

Here are some powerful herbs and essential oils that any household should have:

## Essential Oils for Well-being

LAVENDER
Helpful to reduce stress and anxiety – smell a bunch of lavender or light a scented candle.

## PASSIONFLOWER
Amazing for calming anxiety and helping with sleep problems. It also great for pain relief, heart and menopausal symptoms. If you have attention deficit hyperactivity disorder, passionflower is perfect and it can also be applied to the skin for burns.

## JASMINE
Relieves anxiety and has a sedative effect on nerve cells.

## LEMON BALM
Positive mood booster – add to your bath or unscented body cream.

## CHAMOMILE
Helps to reduce stress – in tea, or put a few drops of an essential oil on a ball of cotton wool and place it under your pillowcase.

## Heavenly Herbs

**Chamomile** – anxiety, sleep and digestive problems.

**Basil** – courage and success in business, brings peace and soothes bad tempers.

**Sage** – aids memory, smudging.

**Lemon Balm** – lunar energy, balances emotions, dispels melancholy, depression.

**Thyme** – purification, fresh start, increases courage and prosperity.

**Mint** – eases digestion, for headaches, increases luck, attracts money and prosperity.

With so much turmoil and stress during these current times, we should look to nature to help us heal physically, mentally and emotionally. However, please remember that your first call should be to consult a doctor!

# Chapter 32

# Pulling It All Together — The Mindful Medium

Being intuitive doesn't mean we are exempt from feeling earthly emotions; we just feel differently. We don't float around in a bubble, untouched by life because we have been given the upper-hand or because we know the answer to every question (including the lottery numbers!), and we certainly don't sail through life. Being psychic doesn't mean we stand above others, we are not better or superior; we have just simply incarnated to serve the Spirit World and we experience everything differently. We have chosen, at soul level, to take on this mission.

When I started out as a medium, I would listen to all the horror stories of the other mediums around me, and at one point I asked myself if I was to continue, would I have to go through the chaos, the troubles, the heartbreak that they did. It was then that I realised (a little word in my ear from a guide) that we have all chosen to incarnate. This conscious choice means we have agreed to feel the rough and the smooth, as it is important we understand and feel these powerful emotions. We are here to experience emotions to help others. If we don't experience a range of emotions, how can we guide others? How can we understand, empathise or recognise people's stories and the stories of their loved ones in spirit? To feel, see, hear or know things may come at a price, but it is necessary. It is part of the deal, the plan, and remember we chose it.

Difficult times which challenge us are initiations, like a test that we must experience in order to grow. They are there also to help us learn and grow, to open our eyes and find solutions. We have agreed to these, they could be health, loss, money, isolation or heart-related, but they ultimately awaken us and inevitably guide us to a realisation which will always be better for our soul.

As we work with Spirit, as we learn to listen, we begin to see the larger picture and we trust that things happen for a reason. Again, it doesn't mean we can rise above them, but knowing Spirit has our best interest at heart, it can soften the journey. All we need to do is listen and be guided, watching for their signs of love and comfort.

## Grounding Exercise

Grounding is especially important to keep your feet firmly planted on the ground. It will give you a sense of being one with the planet and of belonging. Doing this simple exercise will give you disciplined mind energy and direction, which is very important for healing and spiritual work.

*Take three deep breaths and on the in-breath, breathe in all that is good for you, and when you exhale, breathe out any tensions or worries.*

*Focus your attention on your feet and slowly move your awareness up through your legs, thighs, body, arms, neck and head. Be aware of every breath moving in and out, in and out. Imagine that you are surrounded by light. As you breathe in, inhale the light, exhale any tension. Repeat several times. Imagine the light filling your body. As you exhale release any tension from your jaw, your face, your shoulders. Release any tension you may feel from anywhere in your body. Keep inhaling the light and exhaling the tension until you feel calm and relaxed. If your mind begins to drift or fills with mindless chatter, just bring your awareness back to your breathing.*

*Now imagine tiny roots coming out of the bottom of your feet and the bottom of your spine. Feel them growing and growing.*

*Imagine them extending down through the bottom of your chair and through the floor, all the way down through the Earth beneath you. Continue to inhale the light and exhale tension. Imagine these roots wriggling deeper and deeper into the Earth until they reach the Earth's core. Feel the roots taking hold there and connecting you to the centre of the Earth. Visualise the roots expanding, getting bigger and growing stronger. Feel the love you will find there.*

*On the next inhalation, draw the energy of the Earth, up through your roots just as you would draw liquid up through a straw. Draw the energy up through your feet, up your ankles. Feel the energy moving up your legs to your knees. As it continues and reaches your thighs, feel any tension disappear. Move the energy up your spine, and as it reaches your head, you can feel your scalp tingle. You can feel all the parts of your face and your entire body is relaxed and free of tension.*

*Feel the energy move freely around your body, filling your heart. You feel relaxed, calm, peaceful and yet powerful and strong.*

*When you are ready, become aware of your body again, of where you are sitting and the room around you. Feel your breath rise and fall, feel your heartbeat. Listen to all the sounds around you. Wiggle your toes and fingers, and slowly, when you are ready, in your own time, open your eyes.*

### Prayer

*Thank you for guiding me,*
*For being there, shining a light on my path.*

*Thank you for showing me how to weave my gifts,*
*So I can help others understand who they are.*

*Thank you for joining me on my spiritual journey,*
*Supporting me, teaching me and leading me in the perfect direction.*

## Gratitude

*For the people I have met, those I have taught and guided,
I am grateful.*
*To be their mentor and friend, I am honoured.*
*To be a spiritual teacher, a mentor, a healer, a counsellor,
I am blessed.*
*For this opportunity to grow and show others how to grow,
I am thankful.*

## Affirmation

*I am a being of light.*
*I am a seeker of truth.*
*I am connected to the Divine.*
*I have an open heart.*
*I am blessed to be ME.*

My wish now is for you to go forward and find who you are, to step onto your spiritual path and open your heart to the beings of light who are encouraged to work with you.

I wish for you, too, to bring guidance, healing, reassurance to others.

### *Blessings*
*Alison* ♥

# FAQ

### How can you tell if Spirit is around you?

As spirit draw close to us their energy blends and merges with our own. This blend of energy can cause our skin to tingle, our temperature to change with experiences of either warmth or coldness. Sometimes you may experience goosebumps or what feels like cobwebs over your face. Depending on who is blending with me, I can feel emotional, excited, impatient as these are usually the characteristics of the spirit person when they were living. I also get a cold sensation inside my inner ear – this is usually my guides though. Other sensations can be familiar smells, noises, sparks of light or simply a knowing. Sometimes their face or name pops into your thoughts when you haven't been thinking of them, but if you are sensing spirit, it is a good idea to take notice as each loved one will blend with you in a different way.

### How does meditation support your mediumship?

Meditation calms your body and mind so you can clear your thoughts and be more receptive to spirit. By shifting your consciousness, you remove your ego and allow pure communication to take place.

People who meditate do so for different reasons, for mindfulness, to receive messages from spirit and guides in the form of thoughts, images, colours, words or to practise deepening their connection to their Higher Self. This helps us to connect to our truth and be guided by love.

### Can you read for yourself?

Absolutely, but there is a difficulty.

Firstly, if you use a divination tool such as the Tarot or oracle cards, runes or a pendulum then you need to consider how you phrase your question. Asking a yes or no question will stimulate your conscious mind to show you aspects of what your 'ego' wants to hear. By asking a question such as "How will this situation evolve long term?" then you will be shown a clearer outcome.

Another way around interpreting answers to suit your desired outcome is to read the meaning of the card instead of relying on your own interpretation, as again, your ego will manoeuvre your mind and steer you to the answer you wish to receive. Either way, it is safe and helpful to read for yourself if you remain objective and trust the answer, even if it isn't the one you wanted!

## Why do we have both Guardian Angels and Spirit Guides?

Our Guardian Angels are angelic beings who have been with us since the beginning of time. They are higher beings of light which are known as the messengers of God. They have never incarnated on Earth, so although they have infinite wisdom, they are bound by the Universal Laws and can't intervene with our decisions, only being able to support, love, protect and guide us when we ask them, giving them our permission. Guides on the other hand can intervene and it is their role to push us in the right direction. My analogy is that Guardian Angels are like our grandparents who love us unconditionally, look after us and cherish and protect us. Guides are like our parents who whisper to us what to do, hold our hands as we cross the road and offer advice. Like parents, they offer us strength and wisdom, which they lend us when necessary.

Both Guardian Angels and Guides serve us unconditionally and only have our best interests at heart. It is their soul mission to help us grow and to follow our true path. They both hold our soul blueprint closely in their hearts and they both know how to get us there. We are blessed by having both.

## Are dreams really important?

Dreams are wonderful ways of receiving messages, either from your Higher Self or from loved ones and guides. A lot of our dreams are simply processing our thoughts and experiences from everyday life, but they can also bring healing or spiritual grow for our soul. There are around ten different ways to dream. Processing our thoughts and emotions, spirit visitations where we are joined by our loved ones, or other spirits wishing to connect with us or pass on messages, precognitive dreams where we can tap into events which are yet to happen and lucid dreaming where we can change the flow and outcome of what is happening by drifting in and out of the same dream and altering the ending. There are also past life dreams where we can glimpse lives we have lived through in another time period – great for understanding our soul, and dreams where we can either link to someone close through telepathy to communicate or reach out for help. Astral travelling during dreams is where we can visit other places or indeed go to higher dimensions to learn and grow spiritually. All these different dreams have a relevance and are extremely important. To find out what messages your dreams are conveying, try to keep a dream journal, logging the details of the dreams, the messages within them and your emotions. Repeated dreams or recurring dreams are messages to you to take notice. They may not be the same, but the theme (message) will be repeated until you understand and do something about the situation. Lastly, dreams are symbolic, like signs from spirit; watch for symbols and signs, they are key to understanding what your Higher Self is trying to convey.

Dream interpretation is an amazing way to identify how you are feeling emotionally and can give you clues as to how to proceed with a problem or situation.

## How can I tell the difference between a normal dream of a loved one and a visitation?

You will know the difference, trust me!

A processing dream will leave you thinking about what happened, they are often weird, funny or odd in some aspect. My kids laugh at some of my dreams because they are so random. But spirit visitations are something very special indeed. Having one of these dreams is a gift.

You will connect deeply on an emotional and spiritual level. Often the eyes hold the key, they are deep and you may find that you communicate telepathically. There is a deep sense of overwhelming love. I used to dream of my grandpa, for years I had the same recurring dream that I had not seen for ages and never knew why. This was when I was between ten and 25. In my dream I missed him so much, and when I saw him, the love was unbelievable. I don't even remember the content, but the message was simply, "I'm still here and I love you." It was all I needed.

## Which crystals can support your spiritual development?
Oh there are so many; here is my personal list for spiritual awareness, psychic ability, working with the angelic realms, intuition, cleansing your aura and protection.

- Clear Quartz
- Amethyst
- Apophyllite
- Super 7
- Lapis Lazuli
- Labradorite
- Blue Kyanite
- Celestite
- Moonstone
- Galaxite
- Caribbean Calcite
- Spirit Quartz
- Selenite
- Black Obsidian
- Blue Apatite

## Why do we sometimes have a difficult life?

Falling is necessary for spiritual growth.

*Before Alice got to Wonderland, she had to fall!*

There will be times in your lifetime where you feel like you are falling, spiralling into the darkness without a harness. This will feel uncomfortable and scary, but please trust me, you are always being carried even if you can't feel the arms surrounding you or the encouraging words being whispered in your ear.

Our loved ones, angels and guides know that we need to fall sometimes because we gather strength during these times, it is a chance for our soul to explore the depths. Trauma, grief, heartbreak all guide us to question our core beliefs. We search through the darkness, confronting the pain and understanding our inner emotions.

Masking our feelings only lasts a short time before they resurface.

Falling is a journey into yourself. Sometimes we find ourselves pushed, but equally, if we are brave enough, we can jump into the unknown, trusting the Universe has our back.

Once we have landed, however long the falling takes, we arrive with open eyes and clarity of thought. We can finally see the new world around us and appreciate the brightness, the colour, new opportunities.

Falling is difficult, yet it is just a brief time to reconnect to our heart's desires, align our soul and embrace the future.

*Wonderland is only possible once we understand the falling.*

# Final Thoughts...

## Moving Forward in an Uncertain World

Since I started to write this book, many things have changed within the world and indeed with humanity. I truly believe what we have moved through, and are still navigating through, has begun an awakening process in many of us. Compassion has been a keyword with many of us opening our hearts to those suffering, those feeling the burden and to those struggling with stress and anxiety. Many times have I heard beautiful stories about coming together in need, helping and supporting not just family and friends, but communities.

Our amazing Mother Earth has accelerated her ascension process; she is shifting which means we all must try to align with her. We, humanity, are opening up to the concept of LOVE. No longer are we following the rules which bind us and hold us back. Instead we are searching for TRUTH.

Many souls have begun to awaken spiritually too. Questions are being asked about the meaning of life and what happens after we or our loved ones die. They are beginning to explore the possibilities of continued life after death and are turning to a faith or spirituality for answers. I have had the pleasure of speaking with so many people who have come to me for support, guidance and reassurance, helping them and proving to them, through evidence, that we transcend life, and that love continues on the other side.

There too has been a massive movement in understanding healing recently. Natural herbal and floral remedies along with Reiki have been accepted worldwide for a long time now, but people are ready to extend their beliefs to new ways of healing.

Healing with the angels, crystals, colour and sound are all high vibrational healing methods which elevate our energy so disease can't latch on. It helps to cleanse and clear the lower energies, keeping us in a purer state of health. Many people believe that healing is for the physical body, sometimes only when we are ill or in pain; however, healing is also a prevention. We can make sure we are healthy in our body, mind, emotional and spiritual bodies too. In fact, for me this is paramount, and should be part of your daily routine like eating healthily and brushing your teeth. Over the last few years, we have seen anxiety and stress rising; healing and meditation are fantastic tools to use to keep our emotions at bay, after all, it is only when our bodies sink into negativity, that illness will enter our physical body or we become disconnected with ourselves and the world around us.

Positivity, affirmations, healing, raising your vibrations, connecting with your loved ones, guides and angels along with understanding who you really are and what your soul purpose and gifts are, are all ways to help you navigate the changes which we are facing in our uncertain world.

A new world is being born, humanity is awakening, and together with LOVE, GRACE, UNDERSTANDING, COMPASSION, HEALING, BELIEF and TRUST, we can all move forward together in peace.

### Time Is a Movement of Space
*Time ceases to exist.*
*It suspends and flows,*
*Through emotions and desires.*

*Time bends, warps, creates,*
*Opportunities for growth and understanding*
*Who we are.*

*Time has time,*
*Each moment is precious.*
*It guides us, transforms our being.*

*Time calls to explore, develop*
*Evolve and expand.*
*It's our home, Mother Earth.*

*Our choices are thoughts.*
*They guide us,*
*We learn through them.*

*It's time to connect to our soul, our purpose.*
*Revise our plans,*
*Align our hearts.*

*We are one,*
*From source.*

*Feel our hearts beat simultaneously,*
*Sense our rhythm,*
*The flow of life.*

*Allow our voice to speak*
*Express how we feel*
*Never doubt the reason.*

*Be free.*
*Be determined.*
*Be love.*

6TH
BOOKS

**ALL THINGS PARANORMAL**

Investigations, explanations and deliberations on the paranormal, supernatural, explainable or unexplainable. 6th Books seeks to give answers while nourishing the soul: whether making use of the scientific model or anecdotal and fun, but always beautifully written.
Titles cover everything within parapsychology: how to, lifestyles, alternative medicine, beliefs, myths and theories.
If you have enjoyed this book, why not tell other readers by posting a review on your preferred book site?

**Recent bestsellers from 6th Books are:**

## The Scars of Eden
Paul Wallis

How do we distinguish between our ancestors' ideas of God
and close encounters of an extraterrestrial kind?
Paperback: 978-1-78904-852-0 ebook: 978-1-78904-853-7

## The Afterlife Unveiled
What the dead are telling us about their world!
Stafford Betty

What happens after we die? Spirits speaking through mediums
know, and they want us to know. This book unveils their world...
Paperback: 978-1-84694-496-3 ebook: 978-1-84694-926-5

## Harvest: The True Story of Alien Abduction
G L Davies

G. L. Davies's most-terrifying investigation yet reveals one
woman's terrifying ordeal of alien visitation, nightmarish
visions and a prophecy of destruction on a scale never
before seen in Pembrokeshire's peaceful history.
Paperback: 978-1-78904-385-3 ebook: 978-1-78904-386-0

## Wisdom from the Spirit World
Carole J. Obley

What can those in spirit teach us about the enduring bond of
love, the immense power of forgiveness, discovering our life's
purpose and finding peace in a frantic world?
Paperback: 978-1-78904-302-0 ebook: 978-1-78904-303-7

## Spirit Release
### Sue Allen
A guide to psychic attack, curses, witchcraft, spirit attachment, possession, soul retrieval, haunting, deliverance, exorcism and more, as taught at the College of Psychic Studies.
Paperback: 978-1-84694-033-0 ebook: 978-1-84694-651-6

## Advanced Psychic Development
### Becky Walsh
Learn how to practise as a professional, contemporary spiritual medium.
Paperback: 978-1-84694-062-0 ebook: 978-1-78099-941-8

## Where After
### Mariel Forde Clarke
A journey that will compel readers to view life after death in a completely different way.
Paperback: 978-1-78904-617-5 ebook: 978-1-78904-618-2

## Poltergeist! A New Investigation into Destructive Haunting
### John Fraser
Is the Poltergeist "syndrome" the only type of paranormal phenomena that can really be proven?
Paperback: 978-1-78904-397-6 ebook: 978-1-78904-398-3

## A Little Bigfoot: On the Hunt in Sumatra
### Pat Spain
Pat Spain lost a layer of skin, pulled leeches off his nether regions, and was violated by an Orangutan for this book
Paperback: 978-1-78904-605-2 ebook: 978-1-78904-606-9

## Astral Projection Made Easy

and overcoming the fear of death Stephanie June Sorrell
From the popular Made Easy series, Astral Projection Made
Easy helps to eliminate the fear of death through discussion
of life beyond the physical body.
Paperback: 978-1-84694-611-0 ebook: 978-1-78099-225-9

## Haunted: Horror of Haverfordwest

G.L. Davies
Blissful beginnings for a young couple turn into a nightmare
after purchasing their dream home in Wales in 1989.
Paperback: 978-1-78535-843-2 ebook: 978-1-78535-844-9

Readers of ebooks can buy or view any of these bestsellers by
clicking on the live link in the title. Most titles are published in
paperback and as an ebook. Paperbacks are available in
traditional bookshops. Both print and ebook formats are
available online.

Find more titles and sign up to our readers' newsletter at
**www.6th-books.com**

Join the 6th books Facebook group at **6th Books The world
of the Paranormal**